Haunted Holiday Stitches

Spooky and Adorable
Embroidery Designs for
Halloween and Beyond

LAURA McELROY

Haunted Holiday Stitches: Spooky and Adorable Embroidery Designs for Halloween and Beyond

Laura McElroy

catandmagpie.bigcartel.com

Editor: Kelly Reed
Project manager: Lisa Brazieal
Marketing Manager: Koryn Olage
Copyeditor: Linda Laflamme
Interior layout: Danielle Foster
Cover design: Malea Clark-Nicholson
Cover photograph: Laura McElroy

ISBN: 979-8-88814-391-9
1st Edition (1st printing, September 2025)
© 2025 Laura McElroy
All photographs © Laura McElroy

Rocky Nook Inc.
1010 B Street, Suite 350
San Rafael, CA 94901
USA

www.rockynook.com

Distributed in the UK and Europe by Publishers Group UK
Distributed in the U.S. and all other territories by Publishers Group West

Library of Congress Control Number: 2025933667

All rights reserved. No part of the material protected by this copyright notice may be reproduced or utilized in any form, electronic or mechanical, including photocopying, recording, or by any information storage and retrieval system, without written permission of the publisher.

Many of the designations in this book used by manufacturers and sellers to distinguish their products are claimed as trademarks of their respective companies. Where those designations appear in this book, and Rocky Nook was aware of a trademark claim, the designations have been printed in caps or initial caps. All product names and services identified throughout this book are used in editorial fashion only and for the benefit of such companies with no intention of infringement of the trademark. They are not intended to convey endorsement or other affiliation with this book.

While reasonable care has been exercised in the preparation of this book, the publisher and author assume no responsibility for errors or omissions, or for damages resulting from the use of the information contained herein or from the use of the discs or programs that may accompany it.

This book is printed on acid-free paper.
Printed in Korea.

HAUNTED HOLIDAY
Stitches

Spooky and Adorable Embroidery Designs for Halloween and Beyond

LAURA McELROY

*This book is dedicated to my loving husband Jake,
my dearest son Finn, and both my wonderful parents.
Thank you for always encouraging and inspiring me to live my spooky creative
dreams and for your endless love and support for everything I do.
And thank you to all of you who take the time to appreciate my
spooky embroidery work in any way, shape, or form.
I love you all!*

Stitching the Patterns in This Book

*I encourage you to get creative with the patterns in this book! Change the colors, threads, and embellishments however you please. If you'd like to share, I would also love to see your spooky stitching creations. Just tag me (@cat.and.magpie) in your creations on social media, or drop me a message via my website catandmagpie.bigcartel.com.
At the same time, please remember that all the designs shown in this book are copyright protected and are for personal use only. Even if you do decide to alter the patterns and embroideries in any way, they cannot be remade for profit, sold, or redistributed without the express written consent of Laura McElroy and Rocky Nook, Inc.*

Table of Contents

Introduction — xiii

1
Building Your Craft Supply Stash — 1
- Fabric — 1
- Embroidery Hoops — 3
- Embroidery Threads — 4
- Needles — 8
- Scissors — 10
- Pattern Transfer Tools — 10
- Embellishments — 12
- Paints — 14
- Additional Supplies — 16
- Project Supply Shopping List — 19

2
Project Guide — 21
- Setting Up Your Embroidery Hoop — 21
- Transferring Your Pattern — 25
- Painting Fabric with Watercolor Pencils — 30
- Preparing to Stitch — 35
- Finishing Your Embroidery Hoop — 43
- Finishing Touches — 54

3
Stitch Library — 57
- Back Stitch — 62
- Split Back Stitch — 64
- Whipped Back Stitch — 66
- Satin Stitch — 68
- Felt Appliqué — 75
- Stitching Stars — 79
- Leaf Stitch — 83
- Woven Wheel Stitch — 86
- Woven Picot Stitch — 89
- Stitching a Ghost — 92
- Bead and Sequin Embellishment — 94

4
Projects — 105
- Valloween Teacup Bat Pattern — 107
- Haunted Holly Pattern — 111
- Trick or Treat Cupcake Pattern — 115
- Spooky Blue Boo-quet Pattern — 120
- Summer Goth Ice Cream Pattern — 124
- Halloween Pumpkin Cat Pattern — 129
- Krampus Kitty Pattern — 135
- Haunted Garden Ghost Pattern — 139
- Candy Corn Bats Pattern — 144
- Autumnal Witch Hat Pattern — 149
- Seasons Creepings Wreath Pattern — 154
- Code Orange Haunted House Pattern — 159
- Crystal Gazing Ghost Pattern — 164

Acknowledgements — 169

About the Author — 171

Pattern Templates — 173

Introduction

Hello Spooklings!

Welcome to my world of all things spooky and adorable. I'm so happy you have picked up this book and can't wait for you to start stitching up all the embroidery patterns I've created.

My name is Laura, and I'm the artist and creator behind the spooky cute embroidery business Cat & Magpie. From painting and drawing to baking and dressing up, I'm drawn to anything that involves imagination, creativity, and often a little magic! I love cats, spooky films, heavy metal music, being outdoors in nature, searching for hidden treasures in antique shops or vintage markets, and, of course, anything embroidery and Halloween related.

I have loved Halloween for as long as I can remember—the homemade costumes, spooky baking, and trick or treating with family and friends. I have so many wonderful memories of this magical time of year. The desire to keep a little bit of spookiness in my life all year round led to me to launch Cat & Magpie and to write *Haunted Holiday Stitches*. In this book, I'll share my embroidery knowledge, tricks and treats on how I create my designs, and suggestions on the tools and materials you'll need to create your own Halloween-inspired embroideries, so you can bring a little bit of spookiness to your world all year round, too.

As you read and practice, remember: Always explore, play, and push the boundaries of your creativity. Never be afraid to make mistakes on your creative journey. It's so important to learn from and always be inspired by all your past creative selves. Most importantly, just savor each and every step of the process!

Whether you're a beginning crafter or an experienced embroiderer, I hope you'll enjoy *Haunted Holiday Stitches* and learn something new. Be it a new stitch or creative technique, or even just a new artistic perspective, I can't wait for you to bring out your own spooky creative potential. Have fun stitching up all the patterns in this book!

Stay Spooky,
Laura x

1 | BUILDING YOUR CRAFT SUPPLY STASH

Creativity can strike at any time, so I always have a stash of basic craft supplies on hand. In this chapter, I will dive into the craft supplies I use in my work and share some tips to help you build your own stash. I love searching for craft supplies in my local stores and online marketplaces, plus you can find some wonderful treasures in vintage markets and shops, too! The main thing is to have fun exploring the tools and materials available as you discover what you enjoy working with. This chapter also covers everything you will need for the book's projects.

FABRIC

Choosing the right type of fabric to embroider on can seem a bit daunting if you're completely new to the craft, but you'll only need two types for the patterns in this book: natural cotton calico and felt. I prefer a neutral, light-colored fabric background for my designs and art style, but feel free to get creative with other fabric shades and patterns once you get going with the basics!

Natural Cotton Calico

My go-to fabric, natural cotton calico is the base fabric you'll need for all the book's patterns (**FIGURE 1.1,A**). It has a tighter weave, which makes it easier to embroider on. I prefer medium-weight cotton calico for the same reason. Because cotton calico is made with all natural fibers and is free from any bleach or dyes, it also lends itself well to the paint technique I use in my designs (we'll talk about this technique in Chapter 2).

1.1 EMBROIDERY SUPPLIES

1.2 VALLOWEEN CAKE: EMBROIDERY DESIGN FEATURING FELT APPLIQUÉ SKULLS AND HEARTS

Felt

The other fabric I work with is craft felt (**FIGURE 1.1, B**). Craft felt is a synthetic felt, usually made with a blend of acrylic, polyester, or rayon. I use it to add tiny appliqué skulls, hearts, and other elements I want to be raised up off the base fabric (**FIGURE 1.2**). (I'll demonstrate this technique in Chapter 3.) You can buy small sheets of craft felt in craft stores or online, and there's plenty of colors to choose from, as well as glittery felt, which I love! I also use felt to finish the backs of my hoops (I'll explain how in Chapter 2). If you prefer, you can use a wool blend felt instead, which also comes in plenty of color shades.

TIP: *If you want to experiment with stitching on different fabrics, choose ones with a tighter weave first. Silky or looser weave fabrics can be trickier to embroider on. They often require a stabilizing fabric base to make them more manageable and hold the stitched design in place.*

Building Your Craft Supply Stash

EMBROIDERY HOOPS

Embroidery hoops come in many different shapes, sizes, and colors. I use wooden hoops or plastic flexi hoops for my work (**FIGURE 1.1, C**). They are both great for displaying embroidery designs (**FIGURE 1.3**) and are the two types I recommend for the patterns in this book. (Of course, you're welcome to use any type of embroidery hoop you like!)

I'll explain exactly how to set up your hoop in Chapter 2, but the basic approach is simple: All embroidery hoops have an inner and outer ring that you separate and trap the fabric between. I recommend getting to grips with wooden hoops first. They tighten with a screw and tend to hold the fabric tension a little easier than some of the plastic flexi hoops.

TIP: *If you find it too tricky to keep the fabric tension right while using a flexi hoop, stitch your design in a wooden hoop, then swap it into a flexi hoop when you've finished. Make sure you use a wooden hoop that's at least the same size or larger than the flexi hoop you want to display the design in.*

Plastic flexi hoops have a flexible outer ring and a rigid plastic inner ring. You place your fabric over the inner ring and carefully stretch the outer ring back over it. Although fabric can sometimes slip out of place more easily when you're stitching in a flexi hoop, you can easily—and gently!—pull the fabric back into place without having to take the hoop apart.

1.3 SPOOKY TEACUP BATS: EMBROIDERY DESIGN DISPLAYED IN A PAINTED WOODEN EMBROIDERY HOOP & VIOLET TEAPOT GHOST: EMBROIDERY DESIGN DISPLAYED IN A BLACK PLASTIC FLEXI EMBROIDERY HOOP

Building Your Craft Supply Stash

I often like to paint my wooden hoops using acrylic paint and seal them with a layer of clear or glitter Mod Podge glue. Painting a wooden hoop can really add to the overall design of a project, and I absolutely love a glitter finish! Plastic flexi hoops come in a range of colors too, including black, red, pinks, and blues. You can even find faux wood-grain plastic flexi hoops, which is a style of hoop I use a lot. Some of my favorite brands of flexi hoop include DMC, Nurge, Permin, Groves and Banks, and Siesta Frames, which are all available online.

EMBROIDERY THREADS

There's such an array of embroidery threads to choose from; I love haunting my local craft stores in search of new threads to use in my work! When you're building your own thread stash, visit some craft shops in person to get a better idea of what the textures and colors of the different threads look like in real life. You can browse online too, but a photo can only tell you so much. Let's take a look at the thread types you'll need for the designs in this book.

Perle Cotton Thread

Available in multiple thicknesses and a huge range of colors, perle cotton thread (sometimes spelled pearl) is one of the threads I use the most (**FIGURE 1.1, D**). I love the versatility of perle cotton and use it for outlining my designs as well as filling areas in (**FIGURE 1.4**). You can buy this thread in skeins or balls. I work with balls, because I find taking the thread off the spool quicker and easier. Plus, I don't have to worry about getting into thread tangles, which can happen when working from skeins. (Although, I do still get into tangles when one of my cats finds my ball of thread and unravels it all over the house!) If you buy skeins, I recommend winding the thread onto a bobbin before working with it. You can find plain cardboard or plastic bobbins at most craft supply stores, or shop for more durable wooden or decorative ones to build your thread collection. You can also get storage boxes that are designed to hold bobbins of thread to keep your thread collection all neat and organized!

> **TIP:** *Perle cotton comes in four thread thicknesses: 3, 5, 8, and 12. The lower the number, the thicker the thread, and the higher the number, the thinner the thread.*

1.4 GHOSTLY PUMPKIN PATCH: EMBROIDERY DESIGN SHOWING THE USE OF PERLE COTTON FOR OUTLINE STITCHING

1.5 CREEPING IVY PUMPKIN: EMBROIDERY DESIGN SHOWING THE USE OF A SINGLE STRAND OF COTTON TO DEPICT IVY TENDRILS

Stranded Cotton Thread

The most common type of embroidery thread, stranded cotton thread comes in skeins and is made up of six strands, which you can separate to your desired thickness **(FIGURE 1.1, E)**. For my designs, I usually use one strand to create fine tendrils of ivy, delicate cat whiskers, and fine silvery spider webs **(FIGURE 1.5)**. This is a great thread to experiment with too, as you can create lots of stitch textures and effects using different numbers of strands together.

Building Your Craft Supply Stash

TIP: *When you start working from a skein of thread, you always want to pull the thread from the end of the skein with the longer label, as this should stop the thread from getting tangled! Winding the skeins onto bobbins will keep your thread neat and tidy, too.*

Metallic Thread

I love to use sparkly, metallic threads in my work, too. They're great for adding that little bit of eye-catching sparkle to a design, and they've become a firm staple in my craft supply stash. I prefer to work with metallic threads that come on spools, for the same reason I choose to work with balls of the perle cotton thread.

TIP: *When stitching, it's best to work with shorter lengths of thread, as longer threads tend to knot and tangle more easily. Metallic threads can also snag on the fabric as you stitch, which can spoil the piece of thread you're working with. To keep tangles to a minimum, try stitching with thread lengths of no more than 2 feet.*

Metallic threads can be a little trickier to work with and take some practice to get used to. Don't get discouraged; it's inevitable that you'll get your thread in a tangle at some point! When you do get knots and tangles, carefully use the point of your needle to loosen and undo the knot. If the knot refuses to budge, simply cut out the knot with a small pair of sewing scissors. You may need to undo a little of the stitching so you can secure the work you've already done with a new knot, then start again with a new piece of thread. (I'll go into more detail on knots and stitches in Chapter 2.)

The designs in this book mainly use Gütermann or DMC metallic embroidery threads as well as Kreinik Blending Filament threads (**FIGURE 1.1, F**). The DMC metallic threads are ideal for filling in larger areas of sparkle, including moons, bat wings, and haunted house windows, as well as to add line details, such as stars and cobwebs (**FIGURE 1.6**).

Kreinik Blending Filament is very fine and delicate, and I mainly use this metallic thread for cute little ghosts, which you'll notice in many of my designs (**FIGURE 1.7**). There are lots of different sparkly shades of Blending Filament, and the shades I use give my ghosts a lovely iridescent ghostly shimmer. You can use Blending Filament in a single strand, which can take a while to fill in larger areas, or you can combine it in your needle with a strand of perle cotton to create a more subtle sparkle on top of another color. If you want to explore using different metallic threads after trying some of the book's projects, visit your local craft stores to see and feel your options in person, then have fun experimenting to find out what you enjoy working with most!

1.6 CELESTIAL WINTER TEACUP GHOST: Embroidery design showing DMC metallic thread stitch detail

TIP: *While you're stitching, stop every now and then to let your thread unwind to help avoid those unwanted knots and tangles. Simply let the thread you're working with hang downwards, and it'll unwind!*

1.7 HAUNTED MOSS COTTAGE: Embroidery design showing Kreinik Blending Filament stitch detail on the ghost

Building Your Craft Supply Stash

Machine Embroidery Threads

The final type of thread that I use in my work is Gütermann Sew-all Thread (**FIGURE 1.1, G**). This single-stranded embroidery thread comes on spools and is mainly designed for use in a sewing machine. I use it to stitch on beads and sequins, and to secure the fabric in the hoop when I've finished a design. I also use this thread to secure appliqué felt to my designs, matching the thread color to the felt I'm using so it blends in. I use both cotton and polyester machine embroidery thread; polyester is stronger than cotton, so I always use this one to secure the fabric in the hoop. It's fine to use cotton too, but it can break more easily, so just bear this in mind when you're shopping for your supplies. (I'll walk you through how to secure the fabric in Chapter 2.)

NEEDLES

I use various types of sewing needles when working on my designs, including an embroidery or crewel needle, a beading needle, and occasionally a tapestry needle (**FIGURE 1.1, H**). Each type of needle is designed to work best for different techniques, but you'll be using an embroidery needle for most of the stitching techniques in this book. Let's look more closely at each type.

TIP: *Embroidery needle sizes most commonly range from 1–10. The lower the number, the larger (thicker) the needle, and the higher the number, the smaller (thinner) the needle.*

Embroidery or Crewel Needle

Embroidery or crewel needles have slightly elongated eyes to make them easier to thread and have a sharp point to easily pierce the fabric. I use these types of needles the most, as they work perfectly for almost all the stitches I use in my designs.

You can buy packs of assorted embroidery needles, which will give you a good range of sizes. Depending on the thickness of the thread I'm using, I tend to work with size 4, 5, or 7 needles; these will work best for the patterns in this book too.

Building Your Craft Supply Stash

Beading Needle

Beading needles are long, more flexible, and very thin with a smaller eye, which allows them to pass through tiny seed beads. I embellish all my designs with beads, and often sequins too, and the beading needle is the one I use for this job. I use a size 10 or 12 beading needle, which are the most common sizes. The smaller needle eye can be a little trickier to thread, but I use a strand of Gütermann Sew-all Thread as I find it easier to thread into this needle. I also sometimes use a beading needle to attach very small pieces of appliqué felt (**FIGURE 1.8**), as larger needles can spoil the fabric edge; using the fine slender beading needle helps to avoid this mishap!

TIP: *When sewing beads into a design, I often pass the thread through the beads a couple of times to make sure they're well secured to the fabric and to prevent them from moving out of place.*

1.8 ZOMBIE CAKE: EMBROIDERY DESIGN SHOWING THE USE OF DIFFERENT BEADS, SEQUINS, THREADS, AND APPLIQUÉ

Tapestry Needle

Tapestry needles are larger and have a blunt tip, and I use these for a few stitches only, specifically woven stitches when I don't want the needle to pierce or catch on the fabric or thread (see Chapter 2 for details on specific stitches). Tapestry needle sizes work in the same way as embroidery needles, ranging from 13 (larger) to 26 (smaller). I recommend using a smaller size for the patterns in this book, such as size 22 or 24.

Building Your Craft Supply Stash 9

SCISSORS

An essential part of your craft supply stash is a pair of small sewing scissors (**FIGURE 1.1, I**). They're designed with sharp pointed tips to easily and cleanly cut threads close to the fabric you're working on. You can find these scissors in most craft stores, and there's even more to choose from online, including lots of decorative pairs. You can even opt for a lovely vintage pair—just check that they're still sharp enough to snip through your thread!

PATTERN TRANSFER TOOLS

You can transfer a design onto your fabric in multiple ways, from using a simple pencil to a heat-erasable pen to water-soluble stabilizer (**FIGURE 1.9**). Which is best? That depends on your fabric. For example, a pencil or heat-erasable pen works well on light-colored fabrics, but if you're stitching on dark or heavily patterned fabrics, water-soluble stabilizer is a better choice. I've tried other types of pens, including those with water-erasable ink and some whose ink fades over time, but these never worked particularly well for me. Water-erasable pens tend to have thicker nibs, making it harder to get a clear, crisp transfer. The ink that fades away on its own proved to be particularly annoying, especially when I returned to an unfinished project only to find the transfer design had completely disappeared!

To transfer the patterns in this book, you'll need only a heat-erasable pen or a pencil. Next, we'll examine these tools a little closer, and in Chapter 2, I will give you a step-by-step guide on how to transfer patterns.

TIP: *When you use a pencil, bear in mind that you'll need to be very accurate when transferring your design. You won't be able to remove the lines after stitching!*

Pencil

The simplest tool to use to transfer a design onto fabric is a pencil. The only downside is that you won't be able to erase any transfer lines that are still be visible after you finish stitching your design. Make sure you transfer the pattern accurately onto the fabric to avoid any unwanted lines spoiling your finished work!

TIP: *For best results with heat-erasable ink, make sure you're using a setting that's hot enough and keep the hair dryer moving back and forth over the fabric until the lines disappear.*

1.9 Drawing and painting tools

Heat-Erasable Pen

A heat-erasable pen is the ultimate tool for transferring design templates onto light-colored fabric. I discovered these amazing little pens at a craft event almost a decade ago, and they changed the way I transferred my patterns onto the fabric for good! I use a Pilot FriXion heat-erasable pen with the fine 0.7mm tip. The color you choose doesn't really matter; I use black or blue ink because they stand out clearly on the fabric.

When you complete your stitching, you can use a hair dryer to remove any still-visible transfer lines. Be warned, though, that the ink can sometimes reappear on the fabric if the temperature gets very cold. If you do notice any sneaky transfer lines reappearing, simply erase them again with your hair dryer!

Building Your Craft Supply Stash

Water-Soluble Stabilizer

Made from fibers that dissolve when submerged in water, water-soluble stabilizer is useful for transferring designs to dark and patterned fabrics. Whether you use the clear film-like type or the more translucent, paper-like version, the method is the same: Trace your embroidery design on the water-soluble stabilizer with a pen and attach it to your fabric with some small tacking stitches or pins (some stabilizers are even self-sticking). When you finish stitching, submerge your work into water until the fabric stabilizer dissolves.

Although water-soluble stabilizer is perfectly fine to use when you're experimenting with your own design ideas, please *don't* use this transfer method for the patterns in this book! They are not designed to be submerged in water, and you'll risk spoiling the painted elements if you soak them.

EMBELLISHMENTS

I embellish every single design I make with beads, sequins, or a combination of both (**FIGURE 1.1, J**). I've collected small trinkets and treasures to create art with ever since I was a child, and I love visiting craft and bead shops to search for unique and interesting finds. While in college, I began making fairy dolls, decorating their delicate fairy wings using my collection of beads (**FIGURE 1.10**).

Shopping online makes building your own collection easy. There, you can find beads and other embellishments in a huge range of colors and styles. My favorite brand is Mill Hill, and I mainly use seed, Magnifica, and bugle beads in my work, along with sequins.

1.10 VIOLETTA: A FAIRY DOLL I MADE IN 2010, USING FABRIC SCRAPS, WOOL, RIBBONS, AND BEADS

> **TIP:** *As lovely as an old biscuit tin is for storing your beads and sequins, I recommend a simple bead storage container instead. You can buy clear plastic ones online with either small, divided compartments or removable containers. This makes it easier to see what you have when you're working on a project!*

1.11 Jack-o'-lantern Bats: Embroidery design showing background embellishment using seed beads

1.12 Haunted Halloween Cupcake: Embroidery design showing the use of bugle beads to depict cupcake sprinkles

Seed Beads

The smallest type of bead I use in my designs, seed beads are roundish in shape and come in a wide range of colors and unique finishes. Combining different colors together that complement my stitched work, I use Mill Hill Petite Glass Beads (the smallest of the small), Glass Seed Beads, Antique Glass Seed Beads, and Frosted Glass Seed Beads. I use seed beads more than any other type, adding them to backgrounds as tiny stars, to the center of flowers, and as little ghost eyes (**FIGURE 1.11**).

Magnifica Beads

Mill Hill Magnifica Beads are very similar to seed beads but are more cylindrical. They're made of glass and also come in a wide range of colors. I use these beads in the same way I use seed beads, mainly to add background detail to my designs.

Bugle Beads

Available in a variety of colors and finishes, bugle beads are glass cylinders that range from 2mm to 35mm in length. I tend to use shorter bugle beads in my designs; they're perfect for depicting sprinkles on a spooky cupcake, for instance (**FIGURE 1.12**).

Building Your Craft Supply Stash

Sequins

I mainly use small cup sequins on my designs (**Figure 1.1, M**), which are concave, but you can use flat ones too, depending on how you want them to look on the fabric. You can get some really pretty sequins in intricate flower shapes too! I secure my sequins to the fabric with two or three stitches or with beads in their centers (I'll explain various methods in Chapter 3). I tend to work with clear iridescent sequins the most, using them to depict bubbles, suggest glinting ghostly orbs, or give the effect of a shimmery crystal ball (**FIGURE 1.13**).

1.13 Crystal Gazing Ghost: Embroidery design showing the use of sequins to depict a glittering crystal ball

PAINTS

Fabric painting is the other main technique I use in my work. I use paint to fill in larger areas of my designs, which I then stitch upon. You can add color to your fabric using acrylic paints, inks, fabric markers, watercolors, and more. I mainly use watercolors to paint on the fabric and acrylic paint to add color to my embroidery hoops. These are the two types of paint you'll need for the patterns in this book, too.

TIP: *When blending watercolor paint onto your fabric, it's crucial not to add too much water. Add water a little at a time and build your color up gradually, to avoid it bleeding into areas of the design where you don't want it.*

Watercolors

Watercolors apply well to cotton calico fabric, and I prefer using watercolor pencils. They give me more control and help keep each color where I want it to be (**FIGURE 1.14**). Specifically, I use Derwent Academy watercolor pencils for my designs. The patterns in this book call for specific shades of these pencils; however, you can use similar colors from any brand of watercolor pencil you like. Most craft stores sell basic sets.

TIP: *Apply colors to your fabric one at a time and wait for each color to dry before adding another. This helps to avoid the darker colors bleeding into the lighter colors. Always add the black paint last, as this bleeds more easily into other colors.*

Getting used to painting with watercolor can take some practice, but Chapter 2 offers step-by-step advice to help you!

Acrylics

I use acrylic paint to add color to my wooden embroidery hoops (**FIGURE 1.15**). Acrylic paints give good coverage in just one or two coats, and dry quickly too. To keep the finish nice and smooth, apply the paint in thin layers. Any brand of acrylic paint will work, and you can buy these paints from most craft stores.

1.14 SPOOKY SUMMER ICE CREAM: EMBROIDERY DESIGN SHOWING THE USE OF LIGHT AND DARK SHADES OF WATERCOLOR PAINT

1.15 HALLOWEEN PUMPKIN CAT: EMBROIDERY DESIGN DISPLAYED IN A WOODEN EMBROIDERY HOOP PAINTED WITH BLACK ACRYLIC PAINT AND FINISHED WITH PURPLE GLITTER GLUE

Building Your Craft Supply Stash

ADDITIONAL SUPPLIES

We've covered the most important items you'll need for your projects, but a few more tools and supplies can make your work easier (**FIGURE 1.16**). Here are some additional items to add to your craft supply stash:

- SEWING PINS. I use a sewing pin for the woven picot stitch (see Chapter 3). I prefer glass-head pins, which you can buy in packs online or in most craft shops.
- LIGHT BOX. I use a small light box to transfer my designs onto the fabric, but a window will also do the job.
- PAINT BRUSHES. I use a small, fine-tipped paint brush for blending paint onto my fabric, and a small, flat brush to paint my embroidery hoops. You can buy small packs of assorted paint brushes from most craft stores—no need to buy any expensive brushes.
- MOD PODGE GLUE. I use this to seal my painted embroidery hoops. Mod Podge comes in various finishes, including matte, gloss, glitter, and more. I use the gloss and glitter finishes on my hoops. (You can also mix your own glitter into the clear glue.)
- TRACING PAPER. During pattern transfers, this paper allows light to get through when you're tracing the pattern onto the fabric.
- FINELINER PENS. I use these for tracing the patterns onto the tracing paper. You can use a pencil too, if you like.
- TAPE. I recommend using masking tape or washi tape to keep your pattern transfer in place.

Some optional tools that you may want to use include:

- FABRIC SCISSORS. These make cutting out your fabric squares a little easier, but regular scissors are perfectly fine too.
- PINKING SHEARS. These cut in a zigzag line, which can help slow the fraying of your fabric edges while you're stitching.
- NEEDLE THREADER. This handy tool makes threading your needle a little easier.
- NEEDLE MINDER. This decorative magnetic tool keeps your needle safe when you're not using it. Some attach to the fabric you're working on, while others stand alone (**FIGURE 1.1, K**). If you'd rather, you can simply use a pin cushion.
- THIMBLE. I've never actually used a thimble myself, but many embroidery artists wear one to protect the finger they use to push the needle through the fabric (**FIGURE 1.1, L**).

1.16 Magnetic needle minder in the shape of a cat sitting on a cushion and a pair of embroidery scissors, amongst other trimmings

Building Your Craft Supply Stash

PROJECT SUPPLY SHOPPING LIST

Here's a list of all the tools and supplies you'll need for the projects in this book. You should be able to find everything you need in your local craft, art, and fabric shops, or you can check out Etsy, eBay, or independent small businesses online. Being an artist myself, I personally love to shop and support small businesses whenever I can! Finally, don't forget to have a browse around vintage or antique markets for supplies too. You may find some lovely treasures!

Before you shop, however, look ahead at the projects in upcoming chapters, so you know exactly what thread colors and embroidery hoops you'll need to start making the patterns you want to try first.

- Natural cotton calico fabric (medium weight)
- Craft felt (in required shades)
- DMC Perle Cotton (in required shades and thread sizes)
- DMC Six-Strand Embroidery Floss (in required shades)
- Metallic embroidery threads (in required brands and shades)
- Kreinik Blending Filament (in required shades)
- Gütermann Sew-all Thread (in required shades)
- Wooden or plastic flexi embroidery hoops (in required sizes and colors)
- Embroidery needle (size 5 or a mixed size pack)
- Beading needle (size 10)
- Tapestry needle (size 22 or 24)
- Beads (in required types)
- Sequins (in required types)
- Needle minder *or* pin cushion (whichever you prefer)
- Embroidery scissors
- Pilot FriXion heat-erasable pen (black or blue ink)
- Fineliner pen (black ink)
- Tracing paper
- Tape (washi or masking tape)
- Watercolor pencils (in required shades)
- Acrylic paint (if required)
- Mod Podge glue (if required)
- Hair dryer
- Thimble (optional)
- Needle threader (optional)
- Light box (optional)
- Fabric scissors (optional)
- General purpose scissors (optional)

2 | PROJECT GUIDE

Gather your tools and materials. It's time to start your first spooky embroidery project! This chapter will cover everything you need to know to make the designs in this book. I'll walk you step by step through the key phases of a typical project: setting up your embroidery hoop, transferring a design to the fabric, watercolor fabric painting, preparing to stitch, stitching order, and finishing the hoop. Along the way, I'll share some helpful tips and tricks that I've picked up through my years of practice. By the end of the chapter, you'll be well equipped to begin your first project: the Spooky Stitch Sampler (Chapter 3), which is a great way to practice the stitches you'll need for more involved designs (Chapter 4).

SETTING UP YOUR EMBROIDERY HOOP

For the patterns in this book, you'll need both wooden hoops and plastic flexi hoops. As you'll see in Chapter 4, each project lists the type and size of embroidery hoop to use. Find the appropriate one for your project, then cut out a section of cotton calico big enough to fit in your hoop while leaving a few centimeters of extra fabric around the edge. The easiest way to measure how much fabric you need is to simply place your embroidery hoop on top of the fabric and cut out a square around it (**FIGURE 2.2**). If you want to follow along with the examples in this chapter, you'll need a 4-inch hoop.

2.1 (LEFT) CREEPING IVY JACK-O'-LANTERN EMBROIDERY DESIGN
2.2 (ABOVE) MEASURING AND CUTTING THE FABRIC FOR YOUR EMBROIDERY HOOP

Preparing a Wooden Hoop

With your fabric cut, you're ready to add it to your hoop. Here are the steps for a wooden embroidery hoop:

1. Separate the two rings of your hoop by unfastening the screw at the top of the hoop (**Figure 2.3, A**).
2. Place the inner ring on a solid flat surface and place your piece of cotton calico on top of this ring (**Figure 2.3, B**).
3. Place the outer ring on top of the fabric and carefully press down to secure the fabric between the two hoops (**Figure 2.3, C**).
4. Tighten the screw on the outer hoop until the fabric is taught and secure between the two rings, making sure the fabric tension is even and drum-like.

2.3 PREPARING YOUR WOODEN EMBROIDERY HOOP

TIP: *When securing the outer hoop over the inner hoop, you want the outer hoop to be loose enough to fit over the fabric and the inner hoop easily, but not so loose that everything slips around. You can simply tighten or loosen the hoop screw to adjust accordingly.*

TIP: *As you're tightening the screw, keep an eye on how the fabric looks and feels in the hoop. You don't want it to be bunched up or pulled out of shape. Tighten the screw just enough so you can still adjust and smooth out the fabric to the right tension; tighten the screw completely only when you're satisfied.*

Project Guide

2.4 Preparing your flexi embroidery hoop

Preparing a Plastic Flexi Hoop

The method of adding fabric to a flexi hoop is similar:

1. Separate the two rings of your plastic flexi hoop. The outer ring is flexible, so you'll be able to gently remove this from the inner rigid plastic ring (**Figure 2.4, A**)
2. Place the inner plastic ring on a solid flat surface and drape your piece of cotton calico on top of it (**Figure 2.4, B**).
3. Place the outer flexible ring on top of the fabric, carefully stretching it back over the inner hoop to hold the fabric in place (**Figure 2.4, C**)
4. If your fabric tension is not quite right after you've put the flexi embroidery hoop back together, gently adjust the fabric without removing the outer hoop ring until you get the correct surface tension.

> **TIP:** *The flexi embroidery hoops used in the book's patterns have a small metal hanging loop, which is screwed into the top of the outer ring. You can loosen or remove this hanging loop by twisting it, then just screw it back into place once your fabric is secured in the hoop.*

Project Guide 23

TIP: *It can be tricky to keep the fabric tension right when using certain flexi hoops. In my experience, the small and medium round and oval hoops are easier to work in, but the larger and hexagonal flexi hoops don't always hold the fabric secure enough to easily stitch in. If you're having trouble with your fabric tension in a flexi hoop, it's absolutely fine to stitch your design in a wooden hoop instead. Just make sure you use a hoop at least the same size or larger than the flexi hoop in which you plan to display your finished design.*

Painting a Wooden Hoop

If you like, you can paint the outer ring of your wooden embroidery hoop before you add your fabric. I use one or two thin coats of acrylic paint to do this. Any brand of acrylic paint will work, no need to get anything super fancy or expensive! I then seal the paint with a layer of clear or glitter Mod Podge glue (**FIGURE 2.5** and **FIGURE 2.6**)!

TIP: *Some wooden embroidery hoops can be a little rough and rustic looking, so it's a good idea to use some fine grade sandpaper to smooth any splinters and rough edges before you paint them. You can buy sandpaper online or in your local hardware store.*

2.5 (TOP) HALLOWEEN PUMPKIN CAT: EMBROIDERY DESIGN DISPLAYED IN A BLACK-PAINTED HOOP FINISHED WITH PURPLE GLITTER
2.6 (BOTTOM) SPOOKY SKULL TEACUP BATS: EMBROIDERY DESIGN DISPLAYED IN A BLACK-PAINTED HOOP FINISHED WITH IRIDESCENT GLITTER

TRANSFERRING YOUR PATTERN

The next step is to transfer a pattern onto the fabric in your hoop. I prefer transfer methods that use a light source, so I'll take you step by step through two of these approaches. In addition to your prepared hoop, you will need tracing paper, a fineliner pen or sharp pencil, tape, a Pilot FriXion heat-erasable pen, and a light box or natural light source, such as a window (**FIGURE 2.7**).

I'll wrap up by touching upon two methods that are useful for dark fabrics.

You actually need to make two transfers: first from this book's pages to your tracing paper, then from there to your fabric. The patterns provided at the back of this book are all to scale, and I recommend starting with the Spooky Stitch Sampler design, which I created specifically for you to practice the watercolor painting technique and all the embroidery stitches. (If you're confident in your stitches and would rather start with a different design, that's completely fine too!)

Simply place a piece of tracing paper over the design and use a fineliner pen or sharp pencil to trace the design as accurately as you can. Don't worry too much if it's not completely perfect (**FIGURE 2.8**)!

Why not just use the patterns directly from the book? Light sources shine more easily through tracing paper than regular plain paper, making the lines easier to follow on the fabric. You can, of course, skip this step and use the patterns directly from the book; do what works best for you!

2.7 (TOP) PATTERN TRANSFER TOOLS
2.8 (BOTTOM) TRACING PAPER PATTERN TRANSFER

Daylight Transfer Method

One of the simplest methods of pattern transfer is to use a window and daylight! Give it a try:

1. Tape your pattern to a window, so it doesn't slip around while you're tracing (**FIGURE 2.9, A**).
2. Turn your prepared embroidery hoop so the inner ring faces up. This is the side you'll be tracing onto. (Don't worry, you'll flip the fabric before you start to stitch.)
3. Place the embroidery hoop on top of the pattern, making sure the pattern is centered in the hoop (**FIGURE 2.9, B**).
4. Using a FriXion heat-erasable pen, carefully trace the pattern onto the fabric (**FIGURE 2.9, C**).

TIP: *Don't worry if your traced pattern isn't perfectly accurate. You're using the transfer as a guide and can amend any wobbly lines with your stitching. Also, you can heat erase any remaining visible transfer lines after you finish stitching! (See **FIGURE 2.10**.)*

2.9 DAYLIGHT TRANSFER METHOD

2.10 A collection of patterns transferred onto fabric

Project Guide

Light Box Transfer Method

Using a light box or light pad instead of daylight and a window makes transferring patterns a little easier. Not only is the light more reliable (no pausing for passing clouds), but you can also work on a horizontal surface instead of a vertical one. I use a light box, which is simply a wooden structure with a translucent plastic top and a light bulb inside. Light pads are thinner and more compact than light boxes; some enable you to adjust the brightness of the light emitted. The basic transfer steps are similar to the window method:

1. Tape your pattern to the translucent top of the light box, so it doesn't slip around while you're tracing (**FIGURE 2.11, A**).
2. Turn your prepared embroidery hoop so the inner ring faces up. This is the side you'll be tracing onto. (Don't worry, you'll flip the fabric before you start to stitch.)
3. Place the embroidery hoop on top of the pattern, making sure the pattern is centered in the hoop (**FIGURE 2.11, B**).
4. Using a FriXion heat-erasable pen, carefully trace the pattern onto the fabric (**FIGURE 2.11, C**).

2.11 LIGHT BOX TRANSFER METHOD

Project Guide

Pattern Transfer Methods for Dark Fabric

I'm sure you'll want to experiment with stitching on different fabrics at some point, so here are two methods for transferring a design onto dark or patterned fabric that light doesn't shine through easily:

- Use a white dressmaker chalk pencil or white gel ink pen to freehand draw your design directly onto the fabric (**FIGURE 2.12**). Chalk pencil lines can be brushed off, and dressmaker chalk pencils usually come with a little brush specifically for this purpose. If you're using a white gel ink pen, you'll need to be more accurate with your drawing. You likely won't be able to remove the ink once it's on the fabric. On the other hand, if you make any mistakes while drawing, you can always cover them up with a bit of extra stitching!
- Use water-soluble stabilizer to transfer designs onto patterned and dark fabrics (**FIGURE 2.13**). You can freehand draw, trace, or even print your pattern onto the stabilizer, depending on the type you buy. Then, you just apply the pattern directly onto the fabric you want to stitch on. If your water-soluble stabilizer has an adhesive side, simply stick it to the surface of your fabric. If it doesn't, pin or loosely stitch in place. When you finish stitching your design, hold the fabric under warm running water and gently rub the stabilizer away from the stitching until it's completely dissolved. A few brands to look for are Sulky Fabri-Solvy and Sticky Fabri-Solvy, New brothread Wash Away, and DMC Magic Paper.

2.12 Using a chalk pencil to freehand draw a design onto fabric

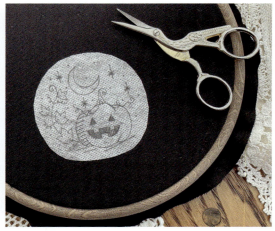

2.13 Using water-soluble stabilizer to transfer a design onto fabric

Project Guide

TIP: *For embroidery designs that involve the use of watercolor paint, stick to light source transfer methods. Any methods that use water to erase the pattern transfer will spoil all the lovely paint detail you spent time working on!*

PAINTING FABRIC WITH WATERCOLOR PENCILS

With the pattern on your fabric, you're ready to add any necessary color to your design using watercolor pencils—one of my favorite parts of the creative process. In addition to your prepared hoop design, gather all the necessary watercolor pencils for the project you're working on (check the project material lists in Chapters 3 and 4 for the colors), a small, fine-tip paint brush, a cup of water, and some paper towels or an old cloth (**FIGURE 2.14**). Finally, pick a flat work surface that you don't mind getting a little paint on! Ready? Then let's get started.

2.14 Fabric painting tools and materials

30   *Project Guide*

2.15 A COLLECTION OF PAINTED DESIGNS READY TO EMBROIDER

How to Paint a Jack-o'-lantern

To demonstrate the watercolor pencil technique, I'll use the Spooky Stitch Sampler design. The watercolor pencil colors you'll need for this design are Orange, Deep Red, and Brown. If you'd like to use a different pattern, the techniques will be the same, only the colors will be different (**FIGURE 2.15**).

Project Guide

1. Place your hoop down on your chosen work surface with the pattern design facing up.
2. Always start with your base color: Using an Orange watercolor pencil, fill in the jack-o'-lantern, taking care to stay within the design lines (**FIGURE 2.16, A**).
3. Add some shadows on top of the Orange, applying Deep Red where the shadows would fall (**FIGURE 2.16, B**).
4. Apply a small amount of water to your fine-tip paint brush, dabbing off any excess on a paper towel or cloth. With your damp brush, carefully start blending the Orange and Red together and into the fabric (**FIGURE 2.16, C**). Don't worry if you get some color on the jack-o'-lantern facial features; you'll be stitching over this bit later!

TIP: *To get used to how the watercolors blend on the fabric, practice on some scrap material before diving into your carefully prepared project design.*

It's best not to apply too much water at once, as this can make the colors bleed into areas you don't want it to go. Gradually blend the colors using a little water at a time to avoid this from happening.

If you do get some paint bleeding, gently place a paper towel over the bleed to soak up the color. You can also add some extra water to the bleed before you apply the paper towel to help remove more of the color.

It's not always possible to completely remove a paint bleed, but you can use some extra stitching to hide paint mistakes!

5. Keep adding more Orange and Red, gradually blending them with water until you're happy with how the color looks (**FIGURE 2.16, D**).
6. Wait for this area to dry, then use your Brown watercolor pencil to fill in the jack-o'-lantern stalk. Then add a little water with your brush to blend it into the fabric (**FIGURE 2.16, E**).
7. When you're happy with how the colors are blended, set the pattern aside to dry thoroughly so you'll be ready to start stitching on the guides when you reach Chapter 3. (**FIGURE 2.16, F**).

TIP: *Your paint will look slightly different on the fabric once it's dried. You can always go back and add more color on top if you want the color to be more vibrant.*

2.16 How to paint a jack-o'-lantern

Project Guide 33

Tricks to Make Painting a Treat

When I first started experimenting with this painting technique, I went through a lot of trial and error. To save you some of my frustrations, I want to share some extra tricks to make your experimenting a little easier!

- Painting onto the design before stitching is best, as your embroidery threads can pick up the paint color if you do any stitching first.
- If you're using black and white paint in your design, always start with the white paint and add the black last. Black paint can bleed very easily into other colors, especially lighter colors, and adding the black last can help to avoid this.
- Let each paint color dry before adding another, especially if the colors are right next to each other, as colors bleed into each other more easily when they're wet. Letting each color dry reduces the risk of any unwanted color mixing.
- Building colors up slowly allows you more control over where you position highlights, shadows, or more saturated areas of color (**FIGURE 2.17**). Don't be too heavy handed when you're using the pencils; start off with a light coverage of color—you can always add more.
- If you do want to remove some color, add a little more water to the area and use a paper towel to soak up some of the pigment. You can also lighten or darken areas of color with white, gray, or black watercolor pencils.
- Finally, the most important thing is to enjoy the process and have fun with this technique! Experiment with blending colors together or even changing the colors of a design. Just go with the creative flow, and don't worry about keeping things perfect! The more you practice, the more you'll get the hang of how the technique works for you.

2.17 SUMMER GOTH SUNDAE: EMBROIDERY DESIGN SHOWING THE USE OF WATERCOLOR PENCILS TO CREATE LIGHTER AND DARKER AREAS

2.18 How to flip your embroidery design to the front of your hoop

PREPARING TO STITCH

Now that your painted design is completely dry, it's time to get out your needle and thread! Before you start stitching, check that all your pattern lines are still visible where you've added the paint. Use your Pilot FriXion pen to draw any lines back in if you need to. You'll also need to flip the embroidery design so it's on the front side of your hoop.

Separate the two rings of your embroidery hoop, and remove the fabric (**FIGURE 2.18, A**).

Place the inner hoop ring down on a flat surface, then place your fabric on top with the design facing up (**FIGURE 2.18, B**).

Place the outer hoop ring on top of your fabric and carefully secure it back over the fabric and inner hoop, making sure the design is centered in the hoop (**FIGURE 2.18, C**).

Gather your embroidery needle (in the size you require, size 5 or 7 will be fine) and all the threads you need for the project you've chosen to work on. There's a materials list included with each of the projects in this book, so just look ahead to see exactly what you need. Cut a 2-foot length (roughly an arm's length) of the thread you'll be starting with, which is likely to be DMC Perle Cotton No. 12 310 Black for most of the projects in this book, including the Spooky Stitch Sampler.

Project Guide

Knot Your Thread

Before making any stitches, you must knot the end of your thread. Tie a single knot 1 or 2 centimeters from the end, then tie a second knot on top of the first knot to make it nice and secure. It can be a little difficult to get the second knot to match up with the first one, but here's a little trick that I learned to make tying knots quicker and easier:

1. Hold the end of your thread between your thumb and index finger on your left hand. (I'm right-handed, so you might want to reverse this if you're left-handed) (**FIGURE 2.19, A**).
2. Wind the longer end of thread away from you, around the tip of your index finger a couple of times, keeping the thread held firm between your thumb and index finger (**FIGURE 2.19, B**).
3. With your right hand, hold the long end of thread taut between your thumb and index finger about 2 or 3 centimeters away from your left hand (**FIGURE 2.19, C**).
4. Securely pinch your thumb and index finger together on your left hand and roll your thumb forwards to bring the thread off the top of your index finger. You should now be holding a little loop of twisted thread (**FIGURE 2.19, D**).
5. Take the tip of your middle finger and pinch down on top of the loop (**FIGURE 2.19, E**) and use your right hand to pull the longer end of thread out and away, which will turn the twisted loop into a little knot at the end of your thread (**FIGURE 2.19, F**). Don't worry if the knot looks a little messy, as long as it doesn't pull through your fabric, it really doesn't matter how neat it looks!

You may need a couple of tries to perfect this knot tying technique, but I promise it's worth learning—especially when working with very fine or delicate threads!

TIP: *When working with thin threads, you will need to wind the thread round your finger a few times to make a knot big enough not to pull through the fabric. As long as you wind the thread around your finger at least once, you can wind as many times as you need. Just keep experimenting until you get the knot you want!*

Project Guide

2.19 How to tie a knot at the end of your thread

TIP: *Sometimes the thread can slip out of place when you're winding it round your finger. I usually wet the tip of my index finger, which makes gripping the thread easier.*

TIP: *Your thread can get a little wound up as you twist and turn your needle for stitches, and this can cause unwanted knots and tangles. Every now and then, stop and let the thread hang downwards so it can unwind.*

2.20 THREADING A NEEDLE

Thread Your Needle

Let's focus on the other end now, and thread your needle (**FIGURE 2.20**). If your supply stash includes a needle threader, go ahead and use it (I very rarely do). To make it a little easier to pass the thread through the eye of your needle without a threader, wet the end of your thread to keep it from separating or snagging as you push it through the eye.

Start Stitching

So, you've got your embroidery hoop ready, your design painted, your threads gathered, and your needle threaded; it's now time to start stitching! Sit somewhere comfortable with a good light source, such as by a window to take advantage of the natural light (my preference) or near a nice bright lamp, so you're not straining your eyes as you stitch. If you like, grab a cozy Halloween blanket, your favorite spooky season drink, and a snack (**FIGURE 2.21**). I also like to listen to music, a podcast, or an audio book while I work.

2.21 My perfect stitching spot

Project Guide

You may be wondering where or what to stitch first. We'll discuss how to make the various kinds of stitches in Chapter 3; plus, all the projects in this book feature step-by-step guides broken down into design elements to make the project and each step easy to follow. Here, I'll briefly outline the order in which I most commonly approach a project. (Don't worry, you'll learn and have a chance to practice all the mentioned stitches in the next chapter and the Spooky Stitch Sampler project.)

2.22 Creeping Ivy Jack-o'-lantern: Starting to stitch the design outline

1. I always start with stitching on any felt appliqué, then outline this in perle cotton, using split back stitch or regular back stitch. Then, I outline the design (**FIGURE 2.22, 2.23**) unless there's areas of satin stitch, which I would fill in first, then add the outlines around these areas after.

2. Next, I stitch any metallic thread detail, using satin stitch, split back stitch, or regular back stitch, depending on the design element I'm working on. This includes spooky house windows, crescent moons, magical swirls, ghosts, bat wings, and more (**FIGURE 2.24**).

3. If the design has raised stitches, such as woven wheel or woven picot stitch, I do these stitches last, because getting the working thread stuck is (unfortunately) easy on these types of stitch. I use woven picot stitch to make 3D bat ears, and woven wheel stitch is great for making roses or circular pieces of Halloween candy (**FIGURE 2.25**).

4. To finish off a project, I add extra embellishments with beads and sequins as the design requires (**FIGURE 2.26**).

2.23 STITCHING THE OUTLINE OF AN EMBROIDERY DESIGN
2.24 STITCHING METALLIC DETAIL ON AN EMBROIDERY DESIGN

2.25 EMBROIDERY DESIGN SHOWING THE USE OF WOVEN PICOT STITCH TO MAKE **3D** BAT EARS
2.26 EMBELLISHING AN EMBROIDERY DESIGN WITH GOLD BEADS

TIP: Don't forget to take regular breaks while you're stitching! Get up to stretch, and go outside for fresh air, too. It can be so easy to get completely absorbed in the stitch process while you're sitting in your cozy sewing spot, but it's also important to give your eyes and hands a break. Get the rest of your body moving!

When the weather is good, I love to work on my embroidery projects outside. You don't have to go far, just to your own garden if you have one, or to the park or even a beach. Living in Wales, I'm very lucky to be close to so many lovely places that are perfect for outdoor stitching. There's a lot of rain here though, so I take any sunny opportunity I can to take my work outside!

Project Guide

Secure a Working Thread

When you come to the end of the thread you're working with, you need to secure it at the back of the embroidery hoop. This will stop any of your stitches from coming loose or unraveling. Here's how:

1. Stop stitching with a few centimeters of working thread left and slip your needle underneath one of the stitches at the back of your embroidery hoop (**FIGURE 2.27, A**).
2. Bring your needle back through the loop of thread a couple of times (**FIGURE 2.27, B**).
3. Carefully pull the thread to secure a knot against the fabric and trim off any excess thread with your sewing scissors (**FIGURE 2.27, C**).

Erase Pattern Transfer Lines

If you used a FriXion heat-erasable pen to transfer your pattern, be sure to erase any pattern transfer lines that may still be visible on your finished work. You can easily remove the lines from the fabric using the heat from a hair dryer (**FIGURE 2.28**). Don't forget to use the hair dryer on a hot setting; hold it close to (but not touching) the fabric, and slowly move it back and forth across the surface of your embroidery until you can't see any transfer lines left.

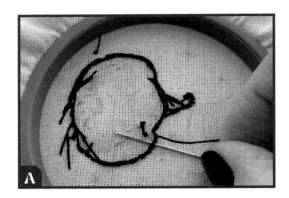

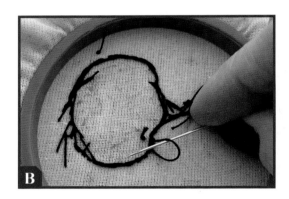

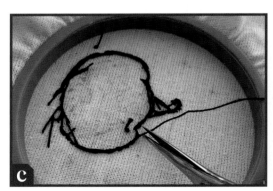

2.27 How to secure your thread at the back of the embroidery hoop

2.28 Completed Creeping Ivy Jack-o'-lantern embroidery

FINISHING YOUR EMBROIDERY HOOP

After you finish stitching your embroidery design, the next step is to close and cover the back of your embroidery hoop so it's ready for you to proudly display on your wall or give to a loved one. Here are a couple of hoop closure methods to try, as well as advice on how to cover your hoop backs.

Thread Closure Method

Using thread is probably the easiest way to close your hoop back; it's the method I always use too. You just need some polyester machine embroidery thread (any color is fine, or you can use a color that matches your fabric if you prefer), an embroidery needle, and a pair of small sewing scissors or fabric scissors.

1. Using your sewing or fabric scissors, trim the fabric around your hoop, leaving about 3 or 4 centimeters of fabric around the edge (**FIGURE 2.29, A**).
2. Cut a length of polyester machine embroidery thread twice as long as the circumference of your hoop plus a few extra centimeters, then match both ends together and thread them through the eye of your needle, leaving a loop at the end (**FIGURE 2.29, B**).

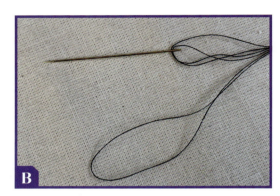

3. Insert your needle from the back, through the fabric near the top of your hoop, then bring it back through the fabric about a centimeter along, passing your needle through the loop at the end of your thread. Pull the thread through to secure the loop to the fabric (**FIGURE 2.29, C**).

4. Keep stitching up and down through the fabric in a running stitch right around the edge of your hoop until you reach your first stitch **(FIGURE 2.29, D–G)**.
5. Now, pull the thread tight so it gathers the fabric in at the back of the hoop **(FIGURE 2.29, H)**.

Project Guide   45

6. Pass your needle through the fabric where your starting stitch is and then bring the needle back through the loop a couple of times, pulling into a knot against the fabric (**FIGURE 2.29, I–J**).

7. You can then pass your needle back under the fabric edge into the back of the hoop and cut the end of your thread to finish (**FIGURE 2.29, K**).

TIP: *The reason I use polyester machine embroidery thread is because it's stronger than cotton and is less likely to break when I gather the fabric at the back of the hoop.*

Attaching the thread to the fabric with a loop stitch instead of a knot works best as knots can be easily pulled out through the fabric as you're gathering it.

2.29 THREAD CLOSURE METHOD

Hot Glue or Tape Closure Method

Another way of closing your embroidery hoop is to secure the fabric at the back using hot glue or double-sided tape. This method can take a little longer and involves a bit more cutting as well as sticking, but it's still a perfectly good way to finish the back of your hoop. You will need a pair of small sewing scissors or fabric scissors, as well as a glue gun or double-sided tape, depending on what you'd prefer to use.

1. Using your sewing or fabric scissors, trim the fabric around your hoop, leaving about 4 or 5 centimeters of fabric around the edge (**FIGURE 2.30, A**).
2. Make cuts in the fabric around the edge of your hoop to make small strips about 2 centimeters wide. Don't worry if they're not all even (**FIGURE 2.30, B**)!
3. If you're using the hot glue method, heat up your glue gun then put a tiny blob of glue on the inner ring of your embroidery hoop directly below one of the strips of fabric you created (**FIGURE 2.30, C**).

Project Guide 47

4. Make sure you wait a few seconds for the glue to cool down a little (you don't want to burn yourself!), then fold the strip of fabric over the inner hoop ring and carefully press it down onto the blob of glue to secure (**FIGURE 2.30, D**). Continue this process until all the strips are stuck down.

TIP: *You can also use a cool or low-melt glue gun, which heats the glue to a lower temperature than regular hot-melt glue guns, reducing the risk of getting a burn. Just be aware that cool-melt glue will also dry quicker than hot-melt glue, so you'll need to be quicker when sticking your strips of fabric down!*

5. If you're using the double-sided tape, cut a small strip of tape and stick it to the inside edge of the inner hoop ring (**FIGURE 2.30, E**).
6. Peel the backing paper off the strip of tape you just applied, then fold the strip of fabric over the inner hoop and press down to secure on top of the tape (**FIGURE 2.30, F-G**). Continue this process until all the strips are stuck down.

2.30 Hot glue or tape closure method

Project Guide

Cover the Back of the Hoop

If you like, you can cover the back of your embroidery hoop to hide away all the messy threads using felt, fabric, or card. This is a completely optional step, but I like to do it. I prefer a nice, neat back to my work, and it provides a space for me to stitch my signature Cat & Magpie labels on the back of each embroidery I make (**FIGURE 2.31**).

To cover the back of my embroidery hoop, I stitch felt over the back using a simple whip stitch. To do so, you will need some felt in your choice of color (I always go for one that complements my embroidery design colors), some thread that matches your felt (I use machine embroidery thread, but perle cotton will work fine too), an embroidery needle, and some sewing scissors or fabric scissors.

2.31 CAT & MAGPIE SIGNATURE LABELS

TIP: *If you plan on covering the backs of all your embroidery hoops, it can be a good idea to create some templates for the different sizes and shapes of embroidery hoop you use regularly. You can make templates with plain paper or card. Simply place the inner ring of your embroidery hoop onto the paper or card and draw around the outside edge of the ring. Cut the template out and you'll be able to use it every time you need to cut out a hoop back.*

Project Guide

1. Cut out a section of felt that's the same size as your inner embroidery hoop ring. The easiest way to do this is to place the inner hoop on top of the felt and draw around the outside edge using a marker pen (**FIGURE 2.32, A**).
2. Cut a length of thread that's the circumference of your inner hoop, plus a few extra centimeters. Tie a knot in one end, and thread your needle (**FIGURE 2.32, B**).
3. Take your needle through the fabric at the edge of your hoop back to secure the knot, then line up your section of felt over the back of the hoop (**FIGURE 2.32, C–D**).

TIP: *If you find it a little tricky keeping your felt in line with the hoop when you begin to stitch it in place, you can always secure it in position first with sewing pins.*

4. Pass your needle through the felt making sure to also catch onto the hoop fabric underneath the felt (**FIGURE 2.32, E**).
5. Repeat this stitch all the way round the hoop to secure the felt in place (**FIGURE 2.32, F**).

TIP: *Another easy way to finish the back of your embroidery hoop is to use card. Simply cut a piece of card to fit the back of your hoop, and stick it onto the edge of the inner hoop ring with hot glue or double-sided tape.*

Project Guide 51

6. Knot your thread when you get back to your fist stitch, then take your needle back through the fabric at the edge of your hoop and out through the felt, cutting the end of your thread here to finish (**FIGURE 2.32, G–J**).

2.32 Covering the back of the embroidery hoop with felt

If you like, you can add an extra touch to your work by either stitching, writing, or printing your name and the date you finished the embroidery on the back of your hoop (**FIGURE 2.33**). Just remember to do this *before* you attach the fabric or card to the back of your hoop!

2.33 Stitched Cat & Magpie signature on the back of my embroidery hoops

FINISHING TOUCHES

You're now ready to proudly display and admire all the hard work you put into your embroidery project! Hang your embroidery up on your wall, display it on a shelf, or place it on the mantel above the cozy log fire (if you have one). It's totally up to you!

If you plan to hang your wooden embroidery hoop designs up, attaching a piece of decorative ribbon or yarn to the hoop screw is a good way to do this (**FIGURE 2.34**). You can even add other decorative items around the embroidery to build your own spooky season gallery wall or mantel display.

2.34 Wooden embroidery hoop design hung up on display with gold yarn surrounded by some little black bats

Project Guide

3 | STITCH LIBRARY

It's time to get spooky stitching!

This chapter will cover all the basic embroidery stitches you need to create the patterns in this book, plus teach you some more advanced stitches that are all useful to have in your repertoire. Specifically, I'll walk you step by step through how to create each stitch, offer tips, and explain where and when to use the stitches in the Spooky Stitch Sampler project. Whether you're new to embroidery or have some experience, this is your opportunity to practice your skills before you get stuck into the patterns coming up in Chapter 4.

You likely already set up your hoop for the Spooky Stitch Sampler design during Chapter 2, but don't worry if you didn't. A full materials list for the pattern follows, as well as a handy stitch guide so you know which threads to use and where in the design to use them. So, grab your embroidery tools, and let's get spooky stitching!

Materials List

- Cotton calico fabric (7-inch square)
- Embroidery hoop (4-inch round wooden or plastic flexi)
- Pattern transfer and transfer tools
- Watercolor painting tools
- Watercolor pencils (Orange, Deep Red, and Brown)
- DMC Perle Cotton No. 12 (310 Black)
- DMC Perle Cotton No. 8 (310 Black, 319 Green, 368 Light Green, 741 Orange, 743 Yellow)
- Kreinik Blending Filament (032 Pearl)
- DMC Diamant Grandé metallic thread (G3821 Gold, G415 Silver, G317 Grey)
- Gütermann Sew-all Thread (800 White, 000 Black)
- White felt
- Mill Hill Glass Seed Beads (00557 Gold and 00161 Crystal)
- Mill Hill Petite Glass Beads (42014 Black)
- Trimits 5mm transparent cup sequins
- Embroidery scissors
- Embroidery needle (size 5)
- Beading needle (size 10)
- Tapestry needle (size 24)
- Black acrylic paint (optional)
- Mod Podge clear glue (optional)

The thread and embellishment brands and colors listed are those I used to create the designs. You can swap them for alternatives if you wish. If you choose to use a wooden hoop, you can paint it using an acrylic paint of your choice and seal with Mod Podge glue.

Stitch Library

Stitch Guide

A. Jack-o'-lantern
- DMC Perle Cotton No. 12 310 Black, split back stitch
- DMC Perle Cotton No. 8 310 Black, satin stitch
- DMC Perle Cotton No. 8 904 Green, back stitch

B. Felt Skull
- Gütermann Sew-all Thread 800 White, whip stitch
- DMC Perle Cotton No. 12 310 Black, back stitch and satin stitch

Stitch Library

C. Ghost
- DMC Perle Cotton No. 12 310 Black, split back stitch and satin stitch
- Kreinik Blending Filament 032 Pearl, back stitch
- Gütermann Sew-all Thread 000 Black, ghost eyes
- Mill Hill Petite Glass Beads 42014 Black, ghost eyes

D. Crescent Moon
- DMC Perle Cotton No. 12 310 Black, split back stitch
- DMC Diamant Grandé metallic thread G3821 Gold, satin stitch

E. Lollipop and Candy
- DMC Perle Cotton No. 8 310 Black, split back stitch
- DMC Perle Cotton No. 8 741 Orange, woven wheel stitch and satin stitch
- DMC Perle Cotton No. 8 743 Yellow, woven wheel stitch

F. Stars and Magic Swirl
- DMC Diamant Grandé metallic thread G3821 Gold, straight stitch and back stitch
- DMC Diamant Grandé metallic thread G415 Silver, back stitch and satin stitch
- DMC Perle cotton No. 12 310 Black, split back stitch

G. Vine and Leaves
- DMC Perle Cotton No. 8 319 Green, whip stitch, leaf stitch
- DMC Perle Cotton No. 8 368 Light Green, whip stitch

H. Bat
- DMC Perle Cotton No. 12 310 Black, split back stitch and woven picot stitch
- DMC Perle Cotton No. 8 310 Black, satin stitch
- DMC Diamant Grandé metallic thread G317 Grey, satin stitch and back stitch

I. Background Embellishments
- Mill Hill Glass Seed Beads 00557 Gold, background detail
- Mill Hill Glass Seed Beads 00161 Crystal, background detail
- Trimits 5mm transparent cup sequins, background detail
- Gütermann Sew-all Thread 800 White, to stitch on the beads and sequins

BACK STITCH

The back stitch is great for outline work, from marking out simple shapes to more intricate design elements. If you're a beginner, it's the ideal stitch to learn first because you'll likely be using it a lot.

BACK STITCH TIPS
- *When doing outline work, try to keep the length of your stitches as even as possible to achieve a nice smooth-looking line.*
- *You can use back stitch to add fine-line details, such as haunted house roof tiles or delicate magic swirls.*
- *You can also use back stitch to add detail to larger areas of a design or even fill areas in, such as the ghosts in several patterns. I'll explain how to use back stitch to fill in these little spooks later in the chapter.*

1. Tie a knot at the end of your thread and bring it up through the back of the fabric with your embroidery needle.

2. Insert your needle back down through the fabric a little further along from where you brought it up, pulling the thread all the way to the back to make your first stitch.

Stitch Library

3. Bring your needle back up through the fabric a stitch length away from where you last took your needle through.

4. Go back down through hole at the top of the last stitch you made, pulling the thread through to the back to make the next stitch.

5. Bring your needle back up through the hole at the top of your last stitch, pulling your thread all the way through to the front.

6. Repeat steps 2 to 5 until you reach the end of the outline you're stitching (or come to the end of your thread) and knot your thread securely at the back of your work.

For the Spooky Stitch Sampler, use back stitch to embroider the magic swirl and the vines at the top of the jack-o'-lantern stalk. Stitch two tiny back stitches for the bat eyes. Later in the project, you'll use this stitch for some of the stars. For now, though, let's go on to the next stitch.

Stitch Library

SPLIT BACK STITCH

As its name implies, the split back stitch is a variation of the back stitch in which you split each stitch with your needle as you work. I use this stitch more frequently than the traditional back stitch, because I prefer the smoother lines it creates when outlining my designs. I also sometimes use it as a fill in stitch too, usually for long thin shapes that I want to fill in with color or metallic thread. The split back stitch is another extremely useful stitch to know, and one of the stitches you'll be using a lot for the patterns in this book.

SPLIT BACK STITCH TIPS
- *Work in small regular stitches rather than longer stitches, because it keeps the line work a little neater, especially when following curves.*
- *When you're stitching a curved design line, use your needle to gently adjust your stitches into place before you split and secure them to the fabric.*

1. Tie a knot at the end of your thread and bring it up through the back of the fabric with your embroidery needle.

2. Insert your needle back down through the fabric a little further along from where you first brought your needle through, pulling the thread all the way to the back to make your first stitch.

Stitch Library

3. Bring your needle back up through the fabric a stitch length away from where you last took your needle through.

4. Take your needle back down through the last stitch you made, which will split the thread, and pull the thread through to the back to make the next stitch.

5. Bring your needle back up through the fabric a stitch length away from the end of your last stitch, pulling your thread all the way through to the front.

6. Repeat steps 4 and 5 until you reach the end of the outline you're stitching (or the end of your thread) and knot your thread securely at the back of your work.

For the Spooky Stitch Sampler, use split back stitch to embroider the black design outlines, starting with the jack-o'-lantern. Later in the project, you'll use split back stitch to outline other elements including the ghost, bat, crescent moon, Halloween candy, and the satin stitch star. Most of these elements require you to work other stitches first before adding in the outline, however, so leave them for now.

Stitch Library 65

WHIPPED BACK STITCH

Another outline stitch, whipped back stitch is worked with two separate threads to create a twisted stitch line. I use this to make flower stems and other lines that I want to look a little more decorative. Using two different colors of thread is the best way to work this stitch, because it really shows off the twist. For a more subtle twisted line, you can use two threads of the same color.

WHIPPED BACK STITCH TIPS
- *Keep your foundation back stitches a nice even length. When you then weave the second piece of thread through these stitches, the result will be a lovely even twist effect.*
- *Use a tapestry needle to weave the thread through your foundation back stitches. The blunt needle tip will enable you to weave the thread without catching the needle point on or snagging the foundation stitches.*

1. Stitch a line of back stitch using your embroidery needle. Keep the stitches an even length, then knot your thread securely at the back of your work.

2. Tie a knot in your contrasting color thread, and using your tapestry needle, bring the contrasting thread up through the hole at the start of your line of back stitches.

Stitch Library

3. Slip your tapestry needle underneath the first back stitch and bring the thread all the way through in one direction.

4. In the same direction, slip your tapestry needle underneath the second back stitch, pulling the thread through again.

5. Continue to slip your tapestry needle through each stitch, always in the same direction (right to left *or* left to right), until you reach the last back stitch in your line.

6. Bring your thread down through the hole at the end of the line of back stitches, and knot securely at the back of your work.

For the Spooky Stitch Sampler, use whipped back stitch to embroider the vine next to the skull.

Stitch Library

SATIN STITCH

An important versatile stitch to add to your embroidery repertoire, satin stitch is used to fill in areas of color. For example, I use this stitch to fill jack-o'-lantern faces, bat wings, crescent moons, haunted house windows, and other small areas.

You can also work satin stitch in different ways, and I often find myself combining methods while I'm working. Don't be afraid to experiment to find out how you prefer to work with this stitch. As long as you've filled in the area you want and you're happy with how it looks, you can't really go wrong!

SATIN STITCH TIPS
- *Think about the direction you want your stitches to go, because their direction can change how the space you're filling in looks, especially large areas. The book's pattern templates include stitch directional lines to help you practice this.*
- *Be careful not to pull your stitches too tight, because tight stiches can pull the fabric out of place and create unwanted bunching.*
- *When I use method one to embroider small areas, such as haunted house windows, I often work the stitch from one side of the shape to the other, instead of starting in the middle.*
- *If you're using satin stitch inside an outlined area, it's best to outline the area after you fill it with satin stitch. Doing so makes it easier to work the satin stitch.*
- *When using method three, you don't have to fan every single stitch from the center hole. Just make sure all your stitches are going in the same direction towards that central point.*

Stitch Library

Method One

I use this method for stitching square or rectangular shapes, such as haunted house windows, or other design elements where I want the stitches to run in a vertical line. This is also one of the most common ways to work a satin stitch.

1. Tie a knot at the end of your thread and bring it up through the back of the fabric with your embroidery needle at the top middle point of your shape.

2. Send your needle back down through the fabric at the bottom of the shape in a vertical line and pull your thread through to create your first stitch.

3. Bring your needle back up through the fabric next to where you first brought your needle through at the top of the shape.

4. Send your needle back down again at the bottom of the shape, creating another vertical stitch next to the first stitch you made.

Stitch Library

5. Repeat steps 3 and 4 until you reach the edge of your shape, then knot your thread securely at the back of your work.

6. Starting with a new piece of thread, repeat steps 1 to 5 to fill in the opposite side of your shape.

For the Spooky Stitch Sampler, use Method 1 satin stitch to embroider the jack-o'-lantern mouth and eyes.

Method Two

I use this method to fill in curved shapes, specifically my crescent moons. As with method one, you start stitching from the middle of your shape. With method two, however, you leave even gaps between each stitch, gradually filling the gaps in as you work. I find this method helps to stop the fabric from bunching or puckering in the center of the crescent shape.

Stitch Library

1. Tie a knot at the end of your thread and bring it up through the back of the fabric with your embroidery needle in the middle inside edge of your crescent shape.

2. Insert your needle back down through the fabric on the outside edge of the crescent directly opposite where you first brought your needle up and pull your thread through to create your first stitch.

3. Bring your needle back up through the fabric a couple of millimeters from where you first brought your needle through.

4. Send your needle back down again on the outside edge of the shape, creating another stitch near to the first stitch you made, following the curve of the crescent.

Stitch Library

5. Repeat steps 3 and 4, evenly spacing your stitches out and following the curve of the crescent until you reach the point of the crescent, then knot your thread securely at the back of your work.

6. Starting with a new piece of thread, repeat steps 1 to 4 for the other side of the crescent, but don't knot your thread when you reach the point of the crescent.

7. Continue to stitch back along the crescent, adding stitches in the middle of each gap between the stitches you've already made.

8. When you reach the other end point of the crescent, stich back along the crescent again, adding stitches to completely fill in the gaps, then knot your thread securely at the back of your work.

For the Spooky Stitch Sampler, use method two satin stitch to embroider your crescent moon, then outline the crescent using split back stitch.

Stitch Library

Method Three

This final method is useful for pointed triangular shapes where you want the stitches to fan out from a single point. I use it to create bats, including their wings and body.

1. Tie a knot at the end of your thread and bring it up through the fabric with your embroidery needle at the point from which you want your stitches to fan out.

2. Send your needle back down through the fabric in the center of the bottom edge of your shape and pull your thread through to create your first stitch.

3. Bring your needle back up through the hole that you first brought your needle through.

4. Send your needle back down again right next to your first stitch and pull your thread through.

Stitch Library

5. Repeat steps 3 and 4 until you reach the edge of your shape.

6. Continue stitching in the same way to fill in the opposite side of your shape, then knot your thread securely at the back of your work.

For the Spooky Stitch Sampler, use method three satin stitch to embroider the bat wings and body, the larger silver star, and the ends of the piece of Halloween candy. Outline the bat wings and body using back stitch or split back stitch.

FELT APPLIQUÉ

I use felt to add another textural element to my designs, and it's a really simple yet effective stitch technique to learn. For the Spooky Stitch Sampler design, you'll be stitching a little appliqué felt skull, using whip stitch to attach the felt to the fabric, and adding the skull detail with back stitch and a little bit of satin stitch for the skull eyes.

FELT APPLIQUÉ TIPS
- *To cut your piece of felt out in the right size and shape, you can trace the appliqué shape from the design pattern onto a piece of tracing paper and cut it out. Place this template on top of the felt, then draw around the template you've made and cut it out.*
- *You can also draw the appliqué shape by eye directly onto the fabric and trim it down to fit the design. Just make sure not to draw the shape too small!*
- *Use your small sewing scissors to cut out your felt shapes and use your Pilot FriXion pen to draw the shape onto the felt so you can erase any visible transfer lines that may be left on your work at the end.*
- *When you're stitching the skull eyes using satin stitch, you can outline your satin stitch with some small back stitches to shape the eyes how you want.*
- *The felt can sometimes look a little fuzzy around the edges once you've finished stitching. Carefully trim any excess felt fluff off using your sewing scissors.*

Stitch Library

1. Trace your skull shape onto the felt, using a template or by eye, and cut out using your sewing scissors.

2. Place your felt skull onto your fabric where you want to attach it.

3. Tie a knot at the end of your thread and bring it up through the fabric with your embroidery needle at the edge of your felt skull.

4. Send your needle and thread back down through the felt skull a couple of millimeters from the edge to create your first whip stitch.

Stitch Library

5. Bring your needle and thread back up through the fabric a few millimeters from where you first brought your needle through at the edge of your felt skull.

6. Repeat steps 4 and 5, following the edge of the felt skull until you reach your first stitch, then knot your thread securely at the back of your work.

7. Using your FriXion pen, draw the skull features onto the felt.

8. Tie a knot at the end of your thread and bring it up through the fabric with your embroidery needle at the edge of your felt skull.

Stitch Library

9. Stitch around the edge of your felt skull using back stitch.

10. Continuing with the same piece of thread, make two small back stitches into the felt to create the skull teeth.

11. Make another two stitches in the felt to create the skull nose.

12. Use satin stitch method one to create the skull eyes, outlining them in back stitch too if you want, then knot your thread securely at the back of your work.

STITCHING STARS

Stars feature a lot in my design backgrounds, and they are very simple to learn how to stitch. I use a few different styles of star in my designs, using a combination of back stitch, simple single stitches, and satin stitch. All three of these star stitch methods are included in the Spooky Stitch Sampler.

STITCHING STARS TIP: *There are so many different ways to depict a star! Feel free to get creative and experiment with creating your own star shapes. Any type of line work stitch can be used here too; as long as you've got the shape and effect you want, there's no right or wrong way to stitch a star!*

Single-Stitch Stars

This is a super simple way of stitching stars: You make four single, straight stitches that overlap each other in the middle.

1. Tie a knot at the end of your thread and bring it up through the fabric with your embroidery needle at the top point of the star.

2. Send your needle back down through the fabric at the bottom point of the star to create your first stitch.

Stitch Library

3. Bring your needle back up through the fabric at the middle-left point of the star.

4. Take your needle back down through the fabric at the middle-right point of the star, creating a stitch that crosses over the first stitch.

5. Bring your needle back up through the fabric at the top-left point of the star.

6. Send your needle back down through the fabric at the bottom-right point of the star, again crossing the middle point of the stitches.

7. Bring your needle back up through the fabric at the top-right point of the star.

8. Take your needle back down through the fabric at the bottom-left point of the star to create your final stitch, then knot your thread securely at the back of your work.

←Back-Stitch Stars

This star shape looks more like a little diamond and is stitched using back stitch.

1. Tie a knot at the end of your thread and bring it up through the fabric with your embroidery needle at the left point of the star.

2. Stitch a line of small back stitches following the shape of the star in a clockwise direction until you reach your first stitch, then knot your thread securely at the back of your work.

Stitch Library 81

Satin-Stitch Stars

Satin stitch is a great way of stitching larger stars that are featured more prominently in a design. I usually do a five-point star shape outlined in back stitch or split back stitch and filled using satin stitch with metallic thread. As always, work your satin stitch first, then add your outline stitch. You can also use this method for any other star shapes too.

1. Tie a knot at the end of your thread and bring it up through the fabric with your embroidery needle at the center of the star.

2. Insert your needle back down through the fabric at the top point of the star to create your first stitch.

3. Bring your needle back up through the hole in the center of the star.

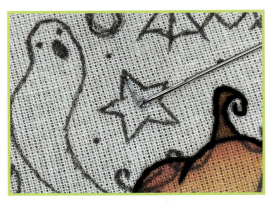

4. Repeat steps 2 and 3, creating a stitch from the center of the star into each point of the star.

Stitch Library

5. Continue to work your way around the star, fanning out your stitches from the edge of the star to the middle point to fill in the gaps, then knot your thread securely at the back of your work.

6. Finally, stitch the outline of the star using split back stitch, then knot your thread securely at the back of your work.

LEAF STITCH

Leaf stitch is made using small diagonal stitches to simulate leaf shapes. You begin with a stitched line down the center of the leaf, then you add stitches that run diagonally from the edge of your leaf to the central line. You can use this stitch for larger or smaller leaf shapes; you'll just be adjusting the number of stitches you need depending on the leaf size.

LEAF STITCH TIPS
- *Working your stitches diagonally from each edge of the leaf to the center gives the leaf more of a center line.*
- *You can also add some extra stitches down the center of your leaf using a different shade of thread to make the central line more prominent.*

Stitch Library 83

1. Tie a knot at the end of your thread and bring it up through the fabric with your embroidery needle at the bottom of the leaf.

2. Embroider a line of split back stitch up the center to the top of the leaf.

3. Bring your needle back up through the fabric at the edge of the leaf close to the top of the leaf on the right side.

4. At a diagonal to the point on the edge of the leaf you came from, insert your needle back down through the central stitch line.

5. Bring your needle back up through the fabric at the edge of the leaf close to the top of the leaf on the left side.

6. Send your needle back down through the central stitch line, again making a diagonal line between your start and end points.

7. Repeat steps 3 to 6 following the shape of the leaf until you reach the bottom of the leaf, then knot your thread securely at the back of your work.

In the Spooky Stitch Sampler, use this stitch to add the four small leaves on the vine next to the skull.

Stitch Library

WOVEN WHEEL STITCH

A really fun stitch to learn, the woven wheel stitch creates a raised circular area of stitches, by weaving thread under and over five foundation stitches that radiate out like spokes of a wheel. This stitch is most commonly used to depict roses, because the way the thread is stitched imitates rose petals. I also use it to create pieces of round Halloween candy and lollipops!

You can adjust the number of spokes in your wheel to three or even seven; as long as you have an odd number of spokes, you'll be stitching in exactly the same way. I prefer to work this stitch using five spokes, which I shall teach you how to do here.

WOVEN WHEEL STITCH TIPS

- Use a tapestry needle to do the woven part of this stitch, because a pointed needle can snag or split your foundation threads as you work, which is not what you want!
- You can use a single shade of thread or use two shades together to create a two-tone effect. You can even buy variegated embroidery thread, which can work really well for this stitch.
- When you're weaving your thread around the foundation stitch spokes, be careful not to pull your thread too tight or the fabric will bunch. You don't want any gaps as you weave either, so just gently pull your thread through as you go so the stitches are nice and close.

Stitch Library

1. Tie a knot at the end of your thread and bring it up through the fabric with your embroidery needle at the center of the wheel.

2. Stitch the five spokes of the wheel with single back stitches working out from the central hole.

3. Bring your thread back up near the central hole of the wheel between two of the spokes.

4. Switch to your tapestry needle, and working in a clockwise direction, slip your needle under the spoke to the right of where you brought your needle up through the fabric, pulling the thread through.

Stitch Library

5. Skip over the second spoke, then slip your needle under the third spoke, pulling the thread through again.

6. Continue to weave your needle under and over the alternating spokes of the wheel until you reach the edge of the spokes.

7. Bring your needle down through the fabric at the edge of the wheel, then knot your thread securely at the back of your work.

For the Spooky Stitch Sampler, use the woven wheel stitch for the lollipop and Halloween candy, then outline them with split back stitch.

WOVEN PICOT STITCH

Another raised woven stitch, woven picot stitch creates little pointed triangles that stand up off the fabric. It's commonly used to depict leaves and is often paired with woven wheel stitch roses. However, you'll be using this stitch to create cute little bat ears! As for woven wheel stitch, a tapestry needle is your best choice for the woven part, and you'll also need a single sewing pin to secure the foundation stitches as you work the stitch. This stitch is a little more complicated and can take some practice to get right, but just persevere and enjoy the process!

WOVEN PICOT STITCH TIPS
- *A long sewing pin with a round top will make it easier to keep your foundation stitches secure as you weave.*
- *Use the tip of your tapestry needle to gently push each woven line into place as you weave. This will keep the thread close together and secure, which is what you want.*
- *When you get to the bottom of the triangle it can get a little trickier to fit the needle under the foundation stitches. If you're left with a space between your picot stitch and the bat's body, just add some extra stitches in to fill the gap.*

1. To prepare for your foundation stitches, pierce your sewing pin down through the fabric at the top point of the triangle, then pierce it back up through the fabric below and away from the edge of the triangle to secure it.

2. Tie a knot at the end of your thread and bring it up through the fabric with your embroidery needle at the bottom-left corner of the triangle.

Stitch Library

3. Securely loop your thread over the top of the sewing pin from left to right, then send your needle back down through the fabric at the bottom-right corner of the triangle, gently pulling the thread through.

4. Bring your needle back up through the fabric at the middle point of the base of the triangle.

5. Securely loop your thread back over the top of the sewing pin from left to right and swap your thread to your tapestry needle. Next, working from right to left, slip your tapestry needle under the right-side stitch, gently pulling the thread through securely to the top of the triangle.

6. Continuing in the same direction, skip over the middle stitch and slip your needle underneath the left-side stitch, gently pulling the thread through again to the top of the triangle.

7. Working from left to right, slip your needle under the middle stitch, gently pulling the thread through and being careful not to pull it too tight. You want the thread to lie flat along the foundation stitches.

8. Continue weaving your thread back and forth, under and over the foundation stitches until you reach the bottom-right corner of the triangle. Make sure to keep the rows of thread close together so there are no gaps in the weave.

9. Insert your needle and thread down through the hole in the bottom-right corner of the triangle, then knot your thread securely at the back of your work.

10. Finally, carefully remove the sewing pin, and you'll be left with a little woven picot stitch.

For the Spooky Stitch Sampler, use woven picot stitch to make both bat ears.

Stitch Library

STITCHING A GHOST

To stitch a ghost, you'll use split back stitch for the ghost outline, a tiny bit of satin stitch for the ghost mouth, and back stitching in Kreinik Blending Filament to fill the ghost. Why back stitch instead of satin stitch? The Blending Filament thread is extremely fine, and I find back stitch just covers the area more securely than a satin stitch would. The iridescent quality of the thread combined with the back stitch also gives the ghosts a lovely shimmer!

STITCHING A GHOST TIPS

- *When you're working with Kreinik Blending Filament, use a short length of thread. This very fine and delicate thread can break and tangle easily as you stitch. Keeping your thread length shorter keeps tangles to a minimum!*
- *When you're filling in the ghost, don't worry about keeping your back stitches all the same length; adjust your stitch lengths to fit around the curves of the ghost shape as you work.*
- *If you have gaps left after you've reached the middle of the ghost, simply go back and add more stitches until you've filled in all the gaps. Remember to keep your stitches flowing in the same direction!*

1. Tie a knot at the end of your Perle Cotton and bring the thread up through the back of the fabric with your embroidery needle at the base of the ghost.

2. Stitch a line of split back stitch all the way around the ghost, then knot your thread securely at the back of your work.

Stitch Library

3. With the same thread, embroider some small satin stitches to make the ghost mouth, then knot your thread securely at the back of your work.

4. Tie a knot at the end of your Blending Filament and bring the thread up through the back of the fabric with your embroidery needle at the base of the ghost. Stitch around the inside edge of the ghost in a clockwise direction using back stitch.

5. Continue to add more lines of back stitch following the shape of the ghost, keeping your back stitch lines close together to fill the area evenly.

6. When you have filled the whole area in, knot your thread securely at the back of your work.

The final step is to add the ghost eyes, which you'll do in the next section.

Stitch Library

BEAD AND SEQUIN EMBELLISHMENT

Once you've completed all the embroidered elements in the Spooky Stitch Sampler, it's time to add some embellishments to the design with beads and sequins. You'll need a beading needle and some Gütermann Sew-all Thread to stitch them to your work. There are many ways to use beads, sequins, and other embellishments, but I'll go through the methods I use, which are also the ones you need to know for the book's patterns.

Most of my design backgrounds are embellished with single seed beads, often used to depict stars or simply to add some extra sparkle!

BEAD EMBELLISHMENT TIPS
- *When you're sewing beads on top of a stitched area, you may need to double stitch them on. They don't always stay in the place you want them to with a single stitch. Simply bring your needle back up to the edge of the bead, thread through the bead again, then take the needle back down through the fabric on the opposite side of the bead to secure at the back of your work.*
- *Some patterns in this book require little clusters of seed beads. These are stitched on in exactly the same way you would a single seed bead, just closer together.*

1. Tie a knot at the end of your thread and bring it up through the fabric with your beading needle at the point where you want to stitch your single seed bead.

2. Thread a single seed bead onto the end of your needle and down onto the thread.

3. Pass your needle back down through the fabric at the very edge of the bead to secure it to the fabric.

4. Repeat this stitch, sewing a single bead onto the fabric at each point shown in the design, then knot your thread securely at the back of your work.

Stitch Library

Stitching Single Bugle Beads

I also use bugle beads to embellish some of my designs, either in the background or in the design itself. Their longer, thinner shape also makes them perfect to depict sprinkles on spooky cupcakes! You stitch these onto the fabric the same way as you do seed beads.

1. Tie a knot at the end of your thread and bring it up through the fabric with your beading needle at the point where you want to stitch your single bugle bead.

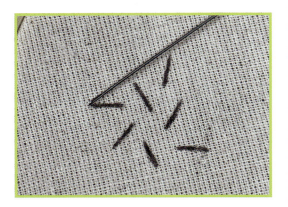

2. Thread a single bugle bead onto the end of your needle and down onto the thread.

3. Insert your needle back down through the fabric at the very edge of the bugle bead to secure it to the fabric, making sure the bead is flat on the fabric and in the direction you want it to face.

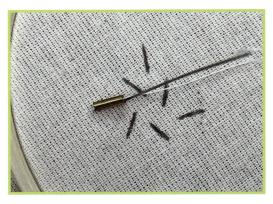

4. Repeat this stitch, sewing a single bugle bead onto the fabric at each point shown in the design, then knot your thread securely at the back of your work.

← *Stitching Seed Bead Eyes*

Seed bead eyes are easy: Sew them in the same way as a single seed bead, but pass your thread through the bead twice rather than once. Because you'll be stitching these beads on top of an already embroidered area, multiple stitches help to keep the beads in exactly the place you want them. I mainly use this method when stitching on any ghost or bat eyes.

1. Tie a knot at the end of your thread and bring it up through the fabric with your beading needle at the point where you want to stitch your first seed bead eye.

2. Thread a single seed bead onto the end of your needle and down onto the thread.

3. Pass your needle back down through the fabric at the very edge of the bead to secure it to the fabric.

4. Bring your needle back up through the fabric at the opposite end of the bead where you first brought your needle up.

Stitch Library

5. Thread your needle through the bead again and back down through the fabric for a second stitch.

6. Repeat this stitch, sewing a second bead on where you want your second eye to be, then knot your thread securely at the back of your work.

✳ Stitching Single Sequins

I often add sequins to my designs, particularly transparent ones that give an iridescent shimmer. I use single sequins as background embellishments, and the transparent iridescent type are perfect for depicting bubbles or shimmery orbs! I stitch single sequins in place by adding a seed bead on top to secure them to the fabric.

1. Tie a knot at the end of your thread and bring it up through the fabric with your beading needle at the point where you want to stitch your single sequin.

2. Thread a single sequin followed by a single seed bead onto the end of your needle and down onto the thread, making sure the sequin sits on the fabric like a cup with the bead in the middle.

3. Pass your needle back down into the fabric through the center of the sequin, pulling your thread through so the seed bead sits in the center of the sequin securing it to the fabric.

4. Repeat this stitch, sewing a single sequin and seed bead onto the fabric at each point shown in the design, then knot your thread securely at the back of your work.

Stitch Library 99

✳ Stitching a Group of Sequins

Sometimes I use a group of sequins to create an area of shimmer. I first used sequins in this way to create the magical window in my first Ouija planchette embroidery design. You'll be using this technique in Chapter 4 when you make the Crystal Gazing Ghost pattern. Here's how to secure the sequins to the fabric:

1. Tie a knot at the end of your thread and starting at the edge of the area you want to fill with sequins, bring the thread up through the fabric with your beading needle.

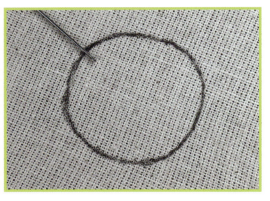

2. Thread a single sequin onto the end of your needle and down onto the thread, so it's up against the fabric.

3. Send your needle back down into the fabric at the edge of the sequin, pulling your thread through to secure.

4. Bring your needle back up through the center hole of the sequin.

100 Stitch Library

5. Pass your needle back down into the fabric at the opposite edge of the sequin, pulling your thread through to secure.

6. Stitch the next sequin on in the same way, slightly overlapping the first one to keep gaps to a minimum.

7. Continue adding sequins, working in a clockwise direction in towards the middle of the area until it's filled in, then knot your thread securely at the back of your work.

SEQUIN EMBELLISHMENT TIPS
- When you're covering an area with a group of sequins, overlap them slightly so you don't get any large empty gaps.
- If you need to change the position of some of the stitches or add extra stitches to attach each sequin, that's completely fine as long as the sequins are all secure against the fabric!

Stitch Library

4 | PROJECTS

Are your fingers itching to stitch a new project? For this chapter, I chose 13 of my favorite designs to help you celebrate spookiness all year round!

Each project includes a visual stitch guide, a materials list, step-by-step instructions, and handy tips. You'll find all the pattern templates at the back of the book. I drew each to scale to fit the hoop size specified in the design's materials list, so you can trace directly from the pages to create your pattern transfers. Be sure to transfer both the pattern's black stitch lines and the orange details that mark where to put embellishments. The patterns' purple lines indicate the directional flow of the stitches for filling in areas, while the gray details indicate the areas you need to paint and will help with shading.

The materials lists detail the brands and colors that I used to create the examples, but you are more than welcome to use alternatives. As long as you're using the specified hoop size, for instance, you can choose any type or color you like. Likewise, feel free to experiment with different colors and styles of thread, beads, and sequins if you want to, as well as to substitute brands that are more readily accessible to you. While gathering your supplies for a project, be sure to check the materials lists for projects you previously completed. Many of the projects use the same threads, beads, and sequins, so you may be able to "shop your stash" for items rather than the store.

I hope you enjoy stitching these designs and getting creative with your work. Experimenting is one of the most exciting parts of the creative process, so don't worry if you don't get the hang of every process or stitch on the first try! Reference the stitch library as often as you need, and don't hesitate to take breaks. Giving your creative batteries time to re-charge is an essential part of the process, too. I can't wait for you to be able to show off your own adorable and spooky creations in your homes and even gift them to your friends and family!

VALLOWEEN TEACUP BAT PATTERN

Valloween—Valentines and Halloween combined—is one of my favorite holiday themes to create some super cute and spooky designs around. The Teacup Bat is one of my simplest and smallest Valloween designs, so it's a perfect pattern to start with, especially for beginners. This design features a pink Valloween teacup adorned with a red felt heart skull, complete with a cute little bat with woven picot stitch ears. If you're still mastering the woven picot stitch, you can always stitch the bat ears using satin stitch instead. Once you've stitched this piece, it'll be the perfect Valloween gift for a loved one!

Materials List

- Cotton calico fabric (6-inch square)
- Flexi embroidery hoop (2.5-inch round; I used a Siesta imitation light wood grain hoop)
- Pattern transfer and transfer tools
- Watercolor painting tools
- Watercolor pencils (Bright Pink and Deep Red)
- DMC Perle Cotton No. 12 (310 Black)
- DMC Perle Cotton No. 8 (310 Black)
- DMC Diamant metallic thread (D5200 White & D310 Black)
- DMC Diamant Grandé metallic thread (G415 Silver)
- Gütermann Metallic Effect Thread (624 Pink)
- Gütermann Sew-all Thread (800 White, 000 Black, and 156 Red)
- Red felt (small piece)
- Mill Hill Petite Glass Beads (40553 Old Rose)
- Embroidery scissors
- Embroidery needle (size 5)
- Beading needle (size 10)
- Tapestry needle (size 24)

Stitch Guide

A. Bat
- DMC Perle Cotton No. 12 310 Black, split back stitch and woven picot stitch
- DMC Perle Cotton No. 8 310 Black, satin stitch
- DMC Diamant metallic thread D310 Black, satin stitch
- Gütermann Metallic Effect Thread 624 Pink, back stitch

- B. Teacup
  - DMC Perle Cotton No. 12 310 Black, split back stitch
  - DMC Diamant metallic thread D5200 White, split back stitch
  - DMC Diamant Grandé metallic thread G415 Silver, back stitch
- C. Appliqué Felt Heart Skull
  - Gütermann Sew-all Thread 156 Red, whip stitch
  - DMC Perle Cotton No. 12 310 Black, back stitch and satin stitch
- D. Embellishments
  - Mill Hill Petite Glass Beads 40553 Old Rose, stitched on with Gütermann Sew-all Thread 800 White and Gütermann Sew-all Thread 000 Black

TIP: *If you don't want to use woven picot stitch for the bat ears, simply work them in satin stitch to match the bat's body and outline in split back stitch.*

Instructions

1. Prepare your embroidery hoop and transfer the Valloween Teacup Bat pattern onto the fabric using your chosen transfer method.
2. Paint the teacup using Bright Pink and Deep Red watercolor pencils. Start off by adding the Bright Pink, then layer on the Deep Red to add some shading. Reference the pattern in the back of the book if you need help with the shading placement.
3. Trace the shape of the heart skull onto the piece of red felt, and cut it out with your embroidery scissors.
4. Attach the felt heart shape onto the fabric in the center of the teacup using whip stitch with a length of Gütermann Sew-all Thread (156 Red).
5. Using DMC Perle Cotton (No. 12 310 Black), stitch around the edge of the heart shape in back stitch, then add the skull features using single back stitches and satin stitch.
6. With a length of DMC Diamant metallic thread (D5200 White), fill in the inside of the teacup using split back stitch, following the directional lines in the pattern at the back of the book.
7. Outline the teacup in split back stitch with DMC Perle Cotton (No. 12 310 Black).
8. Stitch the swirls coming out from the teacup in back stitch with DMC Diamant Grandé metallic thread (G415 Silver). Some of these back stitches will be placed over the top of the stitching you've already done.
9. Using DMC Diamant metallic thread (D310 Black), fill the bat wing sections in with satin stitch. Then fill the body of the bat in with satin stitch using DMC Perle Cotton (No. 8 310 Black).
10. Outline the edges of the bat wings and body with split back stitch using DMC Perle Cotton (No. 12 310 Black).
11. Using Gütermann metallic effect sewing thread (624 Pink), add some single small back stitches to the top of the bat wings, fanning out from the top point of each wing.
12. Make two woven picot stitches for the bat ears using DMC Perle Cotton (No. 12 310 Black).
13. Stitch the Mill Hill Petite Glass Beads (40553 Old Rose) in the background with Gütermann Sew-all Thread 800 White.
14. Add two Mill Hill Petite Glass Beads (40553 Old Rose) for the bat's eyes, stitched on with Gütermann Sew-all Thread (000 Black).
15. Finish the back of your hoop in your chosen method, and remove any remaining visible transfer lines from the front of your work with the heat from a hair dryer.

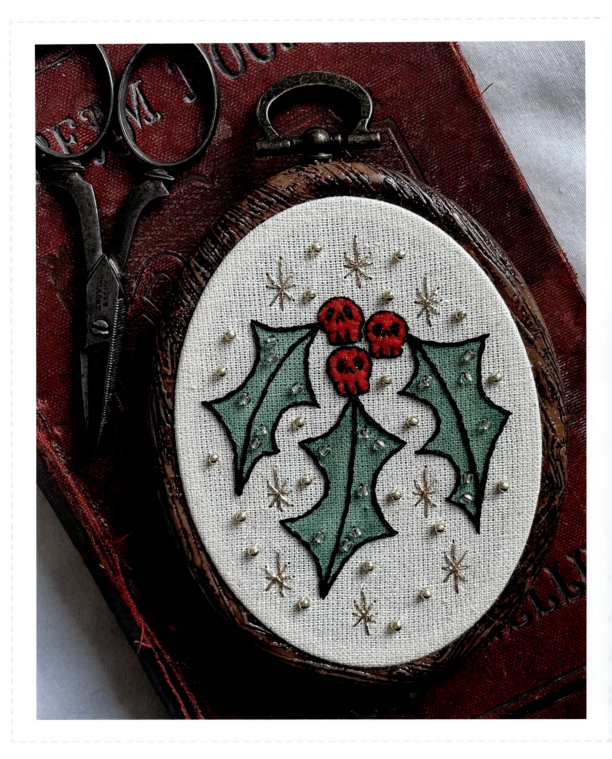

Projects

HAUNTED HOLLY PATTERN

To me, holly is such an iconic piece of winter foliage, especially during the festive season, when you see it adorning homes, decorating yule logs and woven into wreaths. I just had to embroider my own subtly spooky version of this plant by adding some cute little holly berry skulls, marrying the combination of spooky and festive together. This is another design that's perfect for beginners, featuring a spooky sprig of holly surrounded by twinkling stars. Use this pattern to make the perfect piece of spooky winter décor; you could even hang it up as an ornament on your tree!

Materials List

- Cotton calico fabric (6 x 7 inches)
- Flexi embroidery hoop (2.5-x-3.5-inch oval; I used a Siesta imitation dark wood grain hoop)
- Pattern transfer and transfer tools
- Watercolor painting tools
- Watercolor pencils (Dark Green and White)
- DMC Perle Cotton No. 12 (310 Black)
- Kreinik Very Fine Braid thread (221 Antique Gold)
- Gütermann Sew-all Thread (800 White and 156 Red)
- Red felt (small piece; I used red felt with a glitter finish)
- Mill Hill Glass Seed Beads (00161 Crystal and 00557 Old Gold)
- Embroidery scissors
- Embroidery needle (size 5)
- Beading needle (size 10)

Stitch Guide

A. Appliqué Felt Holly Berry Skulls
   - Gütermann Sew-all Thread 156 Red, whip stitch
   - DMC Perle Cotton No. 12 310 Black, back stitch and satin stitch
B. Holly Leaves
   - DMC Perle Cotton No. 12 310 Black, split back stitch
C. Stars
   - Kreinik Very Fine Braid 221 Antique Gold, single stitch stars

D. Embellishments
- Mill Hill Glass Seed Beads 00161 Crystal, stitched on with Gütermann Sew-all Thread 800 White
- Mill Hill Glass Seed Beads 00557 Old Gold, stitched on with Gütermann Sew-all Thread 800 White

Instructions

1. Prepare your embroidery hoop and transfer the Haunted Holly pattern onto the fabric using your chosen transfer method.
2. Paint the holly leaves using Dark Green and White watercolor pencils. Start off by adding the Dark Green, then layer on the White to add highlights and extra Dark Green in the shadows. Reference the pattern in the back of the book if you need help with the shading placement.

3. Trace the shapes of the berry skulls onto the piece of red felt and cut them out with your embroidery scissors.
4. Attach the felt berry skulls onto the fabric in the middle of the holly leaves using whip stitch with a length of Gütermann Sew-all Thread (156 Red).
5. Using DMC Perle Cotton (No. 12 310 Black), stitch around the edges of the berry skulls in back stitch, then add the berry skull features using single back stitches and satin stitch.
6. Outline the holly leaves in split back stitch with DMC Perle Cotton (No. 12 310 Black).
7. Stitch the stars in the background with single straight overlapping stitches using Kreinik Very Fine Braid (221 Antique Gold).
8. Stitch the Mill Hill Glass Seed Beads (00161 Crystal) to the holly leaves with Gütermann Sew-all Thread (800 White).
9. Stitch the Mill Hill Glass Seed Beads (00557 Old Gold) in the background with Gütermann Sew-all Thread (800 White).
10. Finish the back of your hoop in your chosen method and remove any remaining visible transfer lines from the front of your work with the heat from a hair dryer.

TIP: *When you're sourcing your embroidery hoops, the hoop measurements given are usually for the inside dimensions of the hoop. The hoop measurements provided for the patterns in this book follow this convention.*

If you're buying your embroidery hoops from a shop, bring a tape measure with you to check the measurements. If you're buying online, the product listing will usually include a measurement diagram or description provided for reference.

Projects

TRICK OR TREAT CUPCAKE PATTERN

When I was a child, I loved to go trick or treating dressed up in my homemade witch costume. It was a magical time that I look back on fondly with a smile. Now that I'm older and no longer go trick or treating, I love a bit of cozy Halloween baking to get me in the spooky season spirit! The Trick or Treat Cupcake pattern is just one of many of the spooky cake designs I've made over the years. It features my favorite Halloween colors—orange, black, and purple—as well as cute little bat and pumpkin cake toppers, and not forgetting a ghost! So, settle down with your favorite spooky season treats and stitch up this trick or treat cupcake to get you in the Halloween mood!

Materials List

- Cotton calico fabric (6 x 7 inches)
- Flexi embroidery hoop (2.5 x 3.5-inch oval; I used a Permin black hoop)
- Pattern transfer and transfer tools
- Watercolor painting tools
- Watercolor pencils (Black, White, and Purple)
- DMC Perle Cotton No. 12 (310 Black)
- DMC Perle Cotton No. 8 (310 Black and 741 Orange)
- DMC Diamant Grandé metallic thread (G415 Silver & G317 Grey)
- Gütermann Sew-all Thread (800 White and 000 Black)
- Kreinik Blending Filament (032 Pearl)
- Mill Hill Glass Seed Beads (02034 Autumn Flame)
- Mill Hill Magnifica Beads (10006 Eggplant)
- Mill Hill Petite Glass Beads (42014 Black)
- Mill Hill 6mm Small Glass Bugle Beads (72010 Silver Lined Crystal)
- Embroidery scissors
- Embroidery needle (size 5)
- Beading needle (size 10)

Projects

Stitch Guide

A. Cupcake
- DMC Perle Cotton No. 12 310 Black, split back stitch

B. Bat
- DMC Perle Cotton No. 12 310 Black, split back stitch
- DMC Perle Cotton No. 8 310 Black, satin stitch
- DMC Diamant Grandé metallic thread G317 Grey, satin stitch and back stitch

C. Pumpkin
- DMC Perle Cotton No. 12 310 Black, split back stitch and back stitch
- DMC Perle Cotton No. 8 741 Orange, satin stitch

Projects

D. Ghost
   - DMC Perle Cotton No. 12 310 Black, split back stitch and satin stitch
   - Kreinik Blending Filament 032 Pearl, back stitch

E. Stars
   - DMC Diamant Grandé metallic thread G415 Silver, single stitch stars

F. Embellishments
   - Mill Hill Glass Seed Beads 02034 Autumn Flame, stitched on with Gütermann Sew-all Thread 800 White
   - Mill Hill Magnifica Beads 10006 Eggplant, stitched on with Gütermann Sew-all Thread 800 White
   - Mill Hill Petite Glass Beads 42014 Black, stitched on with Gütermann Sew-all Thread 000 Black
   - Mill Hill 6mm Small Glass Bugle Beads 72010 Silver Lined Crystal, stitched on with Gütermann Sew-all Thread 800 White

Instructions

1. Prepare your embroidery hoop and transfer the Trick or Treat Cupcake pattern onto the fabric using your chosen transfer method.
2. Paint the cupcake using the watercolor pencils. Add the Purple to the base of the cupcake, then add a bit more to darken the shadows and use the White to add highlights. Wait for the paint to dry, then paint the top of the cupcake in Black, again adding extra Black to the shaded areas and using the White for highlights. Reference the pattern in the back of the book if you need help with the shading placement.
3. Outline the cupcake in split back stitch with DMC Perle Cotton (No. 12 310 Black).

TIP: If you decide to finish the back of your hoop with felt, you can use any color you like (I like to match the felt to the colors in the design). Stitch your felt backing on using matching or contrasting thread.

4. Using DMC Diamant Grandé metallic thread (G317 Grey), fill the bat wing sections with satin stitch. Then fill the body of the bat in with satin stitch using DMC Perle Cotton (No. 8 310 Black).
5. Outline the edges of the bat wings and body in split back stitch using DMC Perle Cotton (No. 12 310 Black), then stitch two small back stitches to make the bat eyes with DMC Diamant Grandé metallic thread (G317 Grey).
6. Using DMC Perle Cotton (No. 8 741 Orange), fill in the pumpkin with satin stitch.
7. Outline the edge of the pumpkin with split back stitch using DMC Perle Cotton (No. 12 310 Black), then add the pumpkin features on top of your satin stitch using the same thread.
8. Stitch the pumpkin and bat sticks with DMC Perle Cotton (No. 12 310 Black) in split back stitch.
9. Outline the ghost in split back stitch with DMC Perle Cotton (No. 12 310 Black), and add the ghost mouth with the same thread in satin stitch.
10. Fill the ghost in with back stitch using Kreinik Blending Filament (032 Pearl).
11. Stitch the stars in the background with single straight overlapping stitches using DMC Diamant Grandé metallic thread (G415 Silver).
12. Stitch some Mill Hill Glass Seed Beads (02034 Autumn Flame), Petite Glass Beads (42014 Black), and 6mm Small Glass Bugle Beads (72010 Silver Lined Crystal) to the top of the cupcake with Gütermann Sew-all Thread (800 White).
13. Stitch the Mill Hill Magnifica Beads (10006 Eggplant) in the background with Gütermann Sew-all Thread (800 White).
14. Add two Mill Hill Petite Glass Beads (42014 Black) for the ghost eyes, stitched on with Gütermann Sew-all Thread (000 Black).
15. Finish the back of your hoop in your chosen method and remove any remaining visible transfer lines from the front of your work with the heat from a hair dryer.

Projects

SPOOKY BLUE BOO-QUET PATTERN

I'm fascinated by floriography, the language of flowers, and how different combinations of blooms can deliver secret messages and symbolize certain emotions or meanings. The Spooky Blue Boo-quet pattern features some pretty blue roses tied up with a yellow bow adorned with a tiny little felt skull. Despite not occurring in nature, blue roses represent mystery or the unattainable. Whether you're a beginner or an expert embroiderer, this pattern uses just a few stitch techniques to create a detailed and delicate design—perfect for spooky spring!

Materials List

- Cotton calico fabric (6 x 7 inches)
- Flexi embroidery hoop (2.5-x-3.5-inch oval; I used a Permin black hoop)
- Pattern transfer and transfer tools
- Watercolor painting tools
- Watercolor pencils (Dark Blue, White, and Cadmium Yellow)
- DMC Perle Cotton No. 12 (310 Black)
- DMC Perle Cotton No. 8 (319 Green)
- Gütermann Sew-all Thread (800 White and 000 Black)
- White felt (small piece; I used white felt with a glitter finish)
- Mill Hill Glass Seed Beads (02002 Yellow Creme)
- Embroidery scissors
- Embroidery needle (size 5)
- Beading needle (size 10)

Stitch Guide

A. Bow
- DMC Perle Cotton No. 12 310 Black, split back stitch
- Gütermann Sew-all Thread 000 Black, back stitch

B. Appliqué Felt Skull
- Gütermann Sew-all Thread 800 White, whip stitch
- DMC Perle Cotton No. 12 310 Black, back stitch and satin stitch

C. Roses
- DMC Perle Cotton No. 12 310 Black, split back stitch and back stitch
- DMC Perle Cotton No. 8 319 Green, split back stitch and leaf stitch
- Gütermann Sew-all Thread 000 Black, back stitch

D. Embellishments
- Mill Hill Glass Seed Beads 02002 Yellow Creme, stitched on with Gütermann Sew-all Thread 800 White

Instructions

1. Prepare your embroidery hoop and transfer the Spooky Blue Boo-quet pattern onto the fabric using your chosen transfer method.
2. Paint the bow using the Cadmium Yellow watercolor pencil and add highlights using the White. Next, paint the roses using the Dark Blue watercolor pencil, adding extra Dark Blue for the shadows and White for highlights. Reference the pattern in the back of the book if you need help with the shading placement.
3. Trace the shape of the skull onto the piece of white felt, and cut it out with your embroidery scissors.

4. Attach the felt skull onto the fabric in the middle of the bow using whip stitch with a length of Gütermann Sew-all Thread (800 White).
5. Using DMC Perle Cotton (No. 12 310 Black), stitch around the edge of the skull in back stitch, then add the skull features using single back stitches and satin stitch.
6. Outline the bow in split back stitch with DMC Perle Cotton (No. 12 310 Black). Then, using the Gütermann Sew-all Thread (000 Black), add in some single back stitches to the top and bottom inside loops of the bow.
7. Outline the roses in split back stitch with DMC Perle Cotton (No. 12 310 Black) and add the fine-line detail on the petals using Gütermann Sew-all Thread (000 Black).
8. Stitch the rose stems in split back stitch with DMC Perle Cotton (No. 8 319 Green); then, using the same thread stitch the leaves in leaf stitch, following the directional lines in the pattern at the back of the book.
9. Add some small back stitches along the rose stems with DMC Perle Cotton (No. 12 310 Black) to create the tiny thorns.
10. Stitch the Mill Hill Glass Seed Beads (02002 Yellow Creme) in the background with Gütermann Sew-all Thread (800 White).
11. Finish the back of your hoop in your chosen method and remove any remaining visible transfer lines from the front of your work with the heat from a hair dryer.

TIP: *If you can't find the specific color or brand of flexi hoop that I used for a pattern, Vervaco and Nurge offer similar ranges of colored flexi hoops.*

Projects 123

SUMMER GOTH ICE CREAM PATTERN

The heat of summer is not always the best time for us spooky folk who often like to reside in the cool shadows, but I do love venturing out for an evening stroll down the beach with an ice cream cone in hand. The Summer Goth Ice Cream pattern combines my love for both sugary pink hues with a spooky goth aesthetic to create the summer treat of my dreams! This design features a pretty pink and black ice cream decorated with some cute little bats and a sweet sugar skull. There's plenty of stitch techniques in this design as well as lots of sparkly embellishment to enjoy while you're dreaming of Halloween in the late summer sun!

Materials List

- Cotton calico fabric (7 x 9 inches)
- Flexi embroidery hoop (4-x-5.5-inch oval; I used a Permin light pink hoop)
- Pattern transfer and transfer tools
- Watercolor painting tools
- Watercolor pencils (Bright Pink, Deep Red, White, and Black)
- DMC Perle Cotton No. 12 (310 Black)
- DMC Diamant metallic thread (D310 Black)
- Gütermann Sew-all Thread (800 White and 000 Black)
- Kreinik Blending Filament (032 Pearl)
- White felt (small piece; I used white felt with a glitter finish)
- Mill Hill Glass Seed Beads (00161 Crystal, 00145 Pink and 03041 White Opal)
- Mill Hill Petite Glass Beads (42014 Black and 40553 Old Rose)
- Trimits 5mm transparent cup sequins
- The Craft Factory 8mm transparent cup sequins
- Embroidery scissors
- Embroidery needle (size 5)
- Beading needle (size 10)

Projects

Stitch Guide

A. Ice Cream
- DMC Perle Cotton No. 12 310 Black, split back stitch

B. Appliqué Felt Skull
- Gütermann Sew-all Thread 800 White, whip stitch
- DMC Perle Cotton No. 12 310 Black, back stitch and satin stitch

C. Bats
- DMC Perle Cotton No. 12 310 Black, split back stitch and satin stitch
- DMC Diamant metallic thread D310 Black, satin stitch

D. Ghost
- DMC Perle Cotton No. 12 310 Black, split back stitch and satin stitch
- Kreinik Blending Filament 032 Pearl, back stitch

Projects

E. Embellishments
- Mill Hill Glass Seed Beads 00161 Crystal, 00145 Pink, and 03041 White Opal, stitched on with Gütermann Sew-all Thread 800 White
- Mill Hill Petite Glass Beads 40553 Old Rose, stitched on with Gütermann Sew-all Thread 800 White
- Trimits 5mm transparent cup sequins and The Craft Factory 8mm transparent cup sequins, stitched on with Gütermann Sew-all Thread 800 White
- Mill Hill Petite Glass Beads 42014 Black, stitched on with Gütermann Sew-all Thread 000 Black

Instructions

1. Prepare your embroidery hoop and transfer the Summer Goth Ice Cream pattern onto the fabric using your chosen transfer method.
2. Paint the top of the ice cream: First add the White to the relevant sections of the ice cream, referencing the stitch guide image.
3. Wait for the White sections to dry, then fill the remaining ice cream sections in with the Bright Pink watercolor pencil. Notice in the stitch guide image that the pink sections vary in shade, so, add some Dark Red on top of your Bright Pink base to darken the relevant sections and add in some shading.
4. When the ice cream sections are dry, paint the cone using the Black watercolor pencil, adding extra Black for the shadows and White for highlights. Reference the pattern in the back of the book if you need help with the shading placement.
5. Trace the shape of the skull onto the piece of white felt and cut it out with your embroidery scissors.
6. Attach the felt skull onto the fabric at the top right of the ice cream using whip stitch with a length of Gütermann Sew-all Thread (800 White).
7. Using DMC Perle Cotton (No. 12 310 Black), stitch around the edge of the skull in back stitch, then add the skull features using single back stitches and satin stitch.
8. Outline the ice cream and cone in split back stitch with DMC Perle Cotton (No. 12 310 Black). You can use single straight back stitches to add in the lines at the base of the cone.
9. Using DMC Diamant metallic thread (D310 Black), fill the bat's wing sections in with satin stitch. Then fill the bodies of the bats in with satin stitch using DMC Perle Cotton (No. 12 310 Black).

10. Outline the edges of the bat's wings and bodies with split back stitch using DMC Perle Cotton (No. 12 310 Black).
11. Outline the ghost in split back stitch with DMC Perle Cotton (No. 12 310 Black) and add the ghost mouth with the same Perle Cotton in satin stitch.
12. Fill the ghost in with back stitch using Kreinik Blending Filament (032 Pearl).
13. Stitch some Mill Hill Petite Glass Beads (40553 Old Rose) to the top of the ice cream with Gütermann Sew-all Thread (800 White).
14. Stitch the Mill Hill Glass Seed Beads (00145 Pink and 03041 White Opal) in the background with Gütermann Sew-all Thread (800 White). When you're placing these beads, alternate where you place each color so the pink and white beads are evenly distributed across the background.
15. Stitch both sizes of sequin in the background with Gütermann Sew-all Thread (800 White), securing each sequin to the fabric with a Mill Hill Glass Seed Bead (00161 Crystal). Reference the stitch guide image and pattern template for bead and sequin placement.
16. Add two Mill Hill Petite Glass Beads (42014 Black) for the ghost eyes, stitching them on with Gütermann Sew-all Thread (000 Black).
17. For each bat, add two Mill Hill Petite Glass Beads (00145 Old Rose) to make their eyes, stitching the beads on with Gütermann Sew-all Thread (000 Black).
18. Finish the back of your hoop in your chosen method and remove any remaining visible transfer lines from the front of your work with the heat from a hair dryer.

TIP: If you want to lighten any areas of the black ice cream cone, simply add a little more water to the area you want to lighten and gently blot some of the color away using a paper towel. You can use this technique to lighten any other colors you're applying to the fabric too.

Projects

128　　　　　　　　　　　Projects

HALLOWEEN PUMPKIN CAT PATTERN

I'm a cat lover through and through, and I adore my two mischievous kitties, Salem and Loki. I've made countless embroideries inspired by my own cats, in particular Salem, who's a fluffy black cat and a true Halloween icon! This pattern features a spooky black cat perched atop an adorable jack-o'-lantern surrounded by bats, stars, and candy corn. This design will definitely get you in the Halloween stitching spirit!

Materials List

- Cotton calico fabric (8-inch square)
- Wooden embroidery hoop (4-inch round; I used an Elbesee close-grain beech hoop)
- Black acrylic paint
- Fine dark purple glitter
- Mod Podge clear gloss glue
- Pattern transfer and transfer tools
- Watercolor painting tools
- Watercolor pencils (Orange, Deep Red, Brown, and Black)
- DMC Perle Cotton No. 12 (310 Black)
- DMC Perle Cotton No. 8 (310 Black, 904 Green, 550 Purple, 741 Orange, and Blanc White)
- DMC Diamant Grandé metallic thread (G317 Grey)
- Gütermann Metallic Effect Thread (571 Purple)
- Gütermann Sew-all Thread (800 White and 000 Black)
- Mill Hill Glass Seed Beads (02034 Autumn Flame)
- Mill Hill Petite Glass Beads (42039 Brilliant Green)
- Miyuki size 15 seed beads (0181 Galvanized Silver)
- Miyuki size 8 seed bead (209 Fuchsia Lined Crystal)
- Embroidery scissors
- Embroidery needle (size 5)
- Beading needle (size 10)

Projects

Stitch Guide

A. Jack-o'-lantern
- DMC Perle Cotton No. 12 310 Black, split back stitch
- DMC Perle Cotton No. 8 904 Green, back stitch
- DMC Perle Cotton No. 8 310 Black, satin stitch

B. Cat
- DMC Perle Cotton No. 12 310 Black, back stitch, split back stitch
- Gütermann Sew-all Thread 000 Black, back stitch
- DMC Perle Cotton No. 8 550 Purple, satin stitch and split back stitch

C. Bats
- DMC Perle Cotton No. 12 310 Black, split back stitch
- DMC Perle Cotton No. 8 310 Black, satin stitch
- DMC Diamant Grandé metallic thread G317 Grey, satin stitch

D. Candy Corn
- DMC Perle Cotton No. 12 310 Black, split back stitch and back stitch
- DMC Perle Cotton No. 8 550 Purple, 741 Orange, and Blanc White, satin stitch

E. Stars
- Gütermann Metallic Effect Thread 571 Purple, single stitch stars

F. Embellishments
- Mill Hill Glass Seed Beads 02034 Autumn Flame, stitched on with Gütermann Sew-all Thread 800 White
- Mill Hill Petite Glass Beads 42039 Brilliant Green, stitched on with Gütermann Sew-all Thread 000 Black
- Miyuki size 15 seed beads 0181 Galvanized Silver, stitched on with Gütermann Sew-all Thread 000 Black
- Miyuki size 8 seed bead 209 Fuchsia Lined Crystal, stitched on with Gütermann Sew-all Thread 000 Black

Instructions

1. Prepare your embroidery hoop and transfer the Halloween Pumpkin Cat pattern onto the fabric using your chosen transfer method.
2. Paint the jack-o'-lantern using the Orange, Deep Red, and Brown watercolor pencils. First fill the jack-o'-lantern with Orange, then blend with Deep Red into the shaded areas. Wait for this section to dry, then fill in the stalk with the Brown watercolor pencil. Reference the pattern in the back of the book if you need help with the shading placement.
3. Next, paint the cat with the Black watercolor pencil. Start off by filling the cat in with a light layer of the Black, then slowly build up the Black until you're happy with the color saturation and areas of shade.
4. Using DMC Perle Cotton (No. 8 310 Black), stitch the jack-o'-lantern features in satin stitch, then outline the satin stitch features in DMC Perle Cotton (No. 12 310 Black).

5. Outline the jack-o'-lantern and stalk in split back stitch with DMC Perle Cotton (No. 12 310 Black). Using the same thread, stitch the straight lines on the stalk, underneath and on the left side of the jack-o'-lantern with single back stitches.
6. Stitch the jack-o'-lantern vines in back stitch using DMC Perle Cotton (No. 8 904 Green).
7. Using DMC Perle Cotton (No. 8 550 Purple), fill in the top section of the bow using satin stitch, then fill the long bow ends in using lines of split back stitch, following the directional lines in the pattern.
8. Outline the bow and cat in split back stitch with DMC Perle Cotton (No. 12 310 Black). For the shorter lines on the back, tail, and face of the cat, use single back stitches. Add the cat's nose and mouth with some small, closely placed back stitches.
9. Stitch in the fine detail of the cat's whiskers and ears in single back stitches using Gütermann Sew-all Thread (000 Black).
10. Using DMC Diamant Grandé metallic thread (G317 Grey, fill the bat's wing sections in with satin stitch. Then fill the bodies of the bats in with satin stitch using DMC Perle Cotton (No. 8 310 Black).
11. Outline the edges of the bat's wings and bodies in split back stitch using DMC Perle Cotton (No. 12 310 Black).
12. Outline the tiny pieces of candy corn in split back stitch with DMC Perle Cotton (No. 12 310 Black).
13. Referencing the stitch guide image, fill the candy corn pieces in using satin stitch with the relevant colors using DMC Perle Cotton (No. 8 550 Purple, 741 Orange, and Blanc White).
14. Stitch the stars in the background with single straight overlapping stitches using Gütermann Metallic Effect Thread (571 Purple).
15. Stitch the Mill Hill Glass Seed Beads (02034 Autumn Flame) in the background with Gütermann Sew-all Thread 800 White.
16. Add two Mill Hill Petite Glass Beads (42039 Brilliant Green) for the cat's eyes, stitched on with Gütermann Sew-all Thread (000 Black).

17. Add one Miyuki size 8 seed bead (209 Fuchsia Lined Crystal) in the middle of the cat's bow, stitched on with Gütermann Sew-all Thread (000 Black).
18. For each bat, add two Miyuki size 15 seed beads (0181 Galvanized Silver) to make their eyes, stitched on with Gütermann Sew-all Thread (000 Black).
19. Finish the back of your hoop in your chosen method and remove any remaining visible transfer lines from the front of your work with the heat from a hair dryer.

TIPS
- *When you're stitching outlines, it's fine to use a combination of both split back stitch and regular back stitch. I often use single back stitches for straight lines, and for working around smaller curved lines. The more you practice, the more you'll lean into your own personal way of stitching.*
- *For small areas of satin stitch, like the tiny pieces of candy corn in this pattern, I start by outlining the shape first then adding the satin stitch in after.*

Projects

KRAMPUS KITTY PATTERN

A darker tradition of the Christmas season, Krampus is one of my favorite folklore figures—and the inspiration for the adorable Krampus Kitty pattern. The pattern combines the horns and tongue of Krampus with the sweetest black cat wearing a cute, little jingle-bell bow. A super fun and simple festive season design to work on, it uses split back stitch primarily and is decorated with plenty of sparkle, which is perfect for brightening up those long winter nights!

Materials List

- Cotton calico fabric (7-inch square)
- Flexi embroidery hoop (3.5-inch round; I used a Siesta imitation light wood grain hoop)
- Pattern transfer and transfer tools
- Watercolor painting tools
- Watercolor pencils (Deep Red, Yellow Ochre, Cadmium Yellow, White, and Black)
- DMC Perle Cotton No. 12 (310 Black)
- Gütermann Sew-all Thread (800 White and 000 Black)
- Miyuki 3mm bugle beads (0010 Silver Lined Red)
- Miyuki size 15 seed beads (1053 Galvanized Yellow Gold)
- Miyuki size 8 seed beads (910 Red)
- Trimits 5mm gold cup sequins
- Embroidery scissors
- Embroidery needle (size 5)
- Beading needle (size 10)

Stitch Guide

A. Krampus Kitty
   - DMC Perle Cotton No. 12 310 Black, split back stitch, back stitch, and satin stitch
   - Gütermann Sew-all Thread 000 Black, back stitch
B. Embellishments
   - Miyuki 3mm bugle beads 0010 Silver Lined Red, stitched on with Gütermann Sew-all Thread 800 White
   - Miyuki size 15 seed beads 1053 Galvanized Yellow Gold, stitched on with Gütermann Sew-all Thread 800 White

- Trimits 5mm Gold cup sequins, stitched on with Gütermann Sew-all Thread 800 White
- Miyuki size 8 seed beads 910 Red, stitched on with Gütermann Sew-all Thread 800 White

Instructions

1. Prepare your embroidery hoop and transfer the Krampus Kitty pattern onto the fabric using your chosen transfer method.
2. Paint the Krampus kitty bow, tongue, and horns using the Deep Red watercolor pencil. Fill these areas with the Deep Red first, then blend a tiny bit of Black in the shaded areas of the bow. Wait for these sections to dry, then fill in the bell with the Yellow Ochre watercolor pencil, mixing in some of the Cadmium Yellow to give the bell a

more yellow-gold tone. Add a touch of White if you want to add a highlight to the bell and add more Yellow Ochre into the shaded areas.

3. After the bell dries, paint the Krampus cat face: With the Black watercolor pencil, fill in the cat with a light layer of color, then slowly build it up until you're happy with the color saturation and shading. You can add some White if you want to lighten any areas too. Remember, you can reference the pattern in the back of the book if you need help with the shading placement.

4. Outline all of the Krampus kitty design (except the whiskers and the line down the tongue) in split back stitch with DMC Perle Cotton (No. 12 310 Black). You can also use regular back stitches for the small straight lines on the horns and bow. Fill in the cat's nose with a tiny bit of satin stitch.

5. Stitch the Krampus kitty whiskers and line down the center of the tongue with Gütermann Sew-all Thread (000 Black) with single long, straight back stitches.

6. Add a Miyuki size 8 seed bead (910 Red) in the center of each cat eye, stitching them on with Gütermann Sew-all Thread (800 White).

7. Stitch the Miyuki 3mm bugle beads (0010 Silver Lined Red) in the background with Gütermann Sew-all Thread 800 White.

8. Stitch the gold sequins in the background with Gütermann Sew-all Thread (800 White), securing each sequin to the fabric with a Miyuki size 15 seed bead (1053 Galvanized Yellow Gold). Reference the stitch guide image and pattern template for bead and sequin placement.

9. Finish the back of your hoop in your chosen method and remove any remaining visible transfer lines from the front of your work with the heat from a hair dryer.

TIPS
- You'll notice that I use multiple brands of beads across my designs. Don't worry if you can't source the exact brand or shade of a bead that's listed for a project. The most important thing is to match the size of the bead so it fits into the design you're making. Remember, the larger the size number, the smaller the bead.
- The Miyuki brand has a wide range of bugle bead and seed bead sizes, so it's a good brand to shop for when you're sourcing your beads.
- The most common seed bead size is 11, and the Mill Hill beads I use are all this size, except their Petite Glass Beads, which are a size 15.

138 Projects

HAUNTED GARDEN GHOST PATTERN

Wales offers many beautiful gardens to discover, and I'm particularly fond of haunting Bodnant Gardens in North Wales. My husband and I enjoy exploring the rambling rose gardens, magical woodlands, and tranquil streams, and there's plenty of places for bats and ghosts to hide too! Inspired by my love for nature and the outdoors, the Haunted Garden Ghost pattern features a sweet little ghost haunting his own spooky garden. This pattern will certainly bring a touch of summer spookiness to your home!

Materials List

- Cotton calico fabric (6 x 7 inches)
- Flexi embroidery hoop (2.5-x-3.5-inch oval; I used a Siesta imitation light wood grain hoop)
- Pattern transfer and transfer tools
- Watercolor painting tools
- Watercolor pencils (Cadmium Yellow, Orange, Olive Green, and Light Green)
- DMC Perle Cotton No. 12 (310 Black)
- DMC Perle Cotton No. 8 (310 Black, 741 Orange, 904 Green, and 368 Light Green)
- DMC Diamant Grandé metallic thread (G3821 Gold & G317 Grey)
- Gütermann Sew-all Thread (800 White and 000 Black)
- White felt (small piece)
- Mill Hill Glass Seed Beads (02011 Victorian Gold, 02054 Brilliant Shamrock, and 00332 Emerald)
- Mill Hill Petite Glass Beads (42033 Autumn Flame and 42014 Black)
- 5mm flower-shaped sequins (I used a mixed pack of pastel shade flower sequins)
- Embroidery scissors
- Embroidery needle (size 5)
- Beading needle (size 10)

Stitch Guide

A. Skull Flower
- Gütermann Sew-all Thread 800 White, whip stitch
- DMC Perle Cotton No. 12 310 Black, back stitch and satin stitch
- DMC Perle Cotton No. 8 904 Green and 368 Light Green, whip stitch
- DMC Perle Cotton No. 8 741 Orange, back stitch and split back stitch

Projects

B. Skull and Leaves
- Gütermann Sew-all Thread 800 White, whip stitch
- DMC Perle Cotton No. 8 310 Black, back stitch, satin stitch
- DMC Perle Cotton No. 8 904 Green, split back stitch

C. Bats
- DMC Perle Cotton No. 12 310 Black, split back stitch
- DMC Perle Cotton No. 8 310 Black, satin stitch
- DMC Diamant Grandé metallic thread G317 Grey, satin stitch

D. Ghost
- DMC Perle Cotton No. 12 310 Black, split back stitch and satin stitch
- Kreinik Blending Filament 032 Pearl, back stitch

E. Stars
- DMC Diamant Grandé metallic thread G3821 Gold, back stitch

Projects

F. Embellishments
- 5mm flower-shaped sequins, stitched on with Gütermann Sew-all Thread 800 White
- Mill Hill Petite Glass Beads 02034 Autumn Flame, stitched on with Gütermann Sew-all Thread 800 White
- Mill Hill Glass Seed Beads 02054 Brilliant Shamrock and 00332 Emerald, stitched on with Gütermann Sew-all Thread 800 White
- Mill Hill Petite Glass Beads 42014 Black, stitched on with Gütermann Sew-all Thread 000 Black
- Mill Hill Glass Seed Beads 02011 Victorian Gold, stitched on with Gütermann Sew-all Thread 800 White

Instructions

1. Prepare your embroidery hoop and transfer the Haunted Garden Ghost pattern onto the fabric using your chosen transfer method.
2. Paint the flower petals using the Cadmium Yellow watercolor pencil, then blend some Orange in at the base of each petal to create some shading.
3. Paint the leaves using the Olive Green watercolor pencil, then blend some Light Green in at the base of each leaf to create some shading. Reference the pattern in the back of the book if you need help with the shading placement.
4. Trace the shape of the two skulls on the piece of white felt, and cut them out with your embroidery scissors.
5. Stitch both felt skulls onto the fabric using whip stitch with a length of Gütermann Sew-all Thread (800 White). Place the small skull in the middle of the flower and position the large skull at the bottom of the design amongst the leaves.
6. Using DMC Perle Cotton (No. 12 310 Black), stitch around the edge of the small skull in back stitch, then add the skull features using single back stitches and satin stitch.
7. Using DMC Perle Cotton (No. 8 310 Black), stitch around the edge of the large skull in back stitch, then add the skull features using single back stitches and satin stitch.
8. Outline the leaves surrounding the large skull in split back stitch with DMC Perle Cotton (No. 8 904 Green) and do the same for the central line of each leaf.
9. Work the flower stem in whip stitch using DMC Perle Cotton (No. 8 904 Green and 368 Light Green). Use the darker thread for the foundation back stitches and weave the Light Green thread through the back stitches.

Projects

10. Outline the flower petals surrounding the small skull in split back stitch with DMC Perle Cotton (No. 8 741 Orange) and add a single back stitch down the center of each petal in the same thread.
11. Using DMC Diamant Grandé metallic thread (G317 Grey), fill the bat's wing sections in with satin stitch. Then fill the bodies of the bats in with satin stitch using DMC Perle Cotton (No. 8 310 Black).
12. Outline the edges of the bat's wings and bodies with split back stitch using DMC Perle Cotton (No. 12 310 Black), then stitch two small back stitches to make the bat eyes with DMC Diamant Grandé metallic thread (G317 Grey).
13. Outline the ghost in split back stitch with DMC Perle Cotton (No. 12 310 Black) and add the ghost mouth with the same thread in satin stitch.
14. Fill in the ghost with back stitch using Kreinik Blending Filament (032 Pearl).
15. Stitch the stars in the background with back stitch using DMC Diamant Grandé metallic thread (G3821 Gold).
16. For the ghost eyes, add two Mill Hill Petite Glass Beads (42014 Black), stitching them on with Gütermann Sew-all Thread (000 Black).
17. Stitch the Mill Hill Glass Seed Beads (02011 Victorian Gold) in the background with Gütermann Sew-all Thread (800 White).
18. Stitch three flower-shaped sequins at the base of the large skull with Gütermann Sew-all Thread (800 White), securing each sequin to the fabric with a Mill Hill Petite Glass Bead (02034 Autumn Flame).
19. Stitch some Mill Hill Glass Seed Beads (02054 Brilliant Shamrock and 00332 Emerald) around the base of the large skull with Gütermann Sew-all Thread (800 White). Reference the stitch guide image and pattern template for bead and sequin placement.
20. Finish the back of your hoop in your chosen method and remove any remaining visible transfer lines from the front of your work with the heat from a hair dryer.

TIPS

- *Filling in the ghosts with the Kreinik Blending Filament can take quite a long time. If you prefer, you can fill your ghosts in using DMC Perle Cotton No. 8 (Blanc White) combined with a length of the Blending Filament. Just thread your needle with both types of threads and stitch your back stitches in the usual way.*
- *You can also choose to use other types of metallic threads to fill your ghosts in if you want. Have fun experimenting, and see what works best for you!*

Projects

CANDY CORN BATS PATTERN

In the lead up to Halloween, we don't often see candy corn in our shops here in Wales. Despite never tasting this Halloween treat myself, however, I do love a candy corn–themed design. The Candy Corn Bats pattern would be a super adorable addition to any spooky season art display! Bats are also one of my favorite animals, and they frequently fly into many of my embroidery designs. This time two candy corn bats are flying home with their trick or treat pails overflowing with Halloween candy! The pattern calls for woven wheel stitch to make the lollipops, but you could use satin stitch or even paint them in, if you prefer.

Materials List

- Cotton calico fabric (8-inch square)
- Flexi embroidery hoop (4-inch round; I used a Siesta imitation light wood grain hoop)
- Pattern transfer and transfer tools
- Watercolor painting tools
- Watercolor pencils (Orange and Black)
- DMC Perle Cotton No. 12 (310 Black)
- DMC Perle Cotton No. 8 (743 Yellow, 741 Orange, and Blanc White)
- Gütermann Sew-all Thread (800 White and 000 Black)
- Mill Hill Petite Glass Beads (42033 Autumn Flame and 42014 Black)
- Miyuki size 11 seed beads (422 Opaque Yellow Luster and 402 Opaque White)
- Embroidery scissors
- Embroidery needle (size 5)
- Beading needle (size 10)

Stitch Guide

A. Bats
- DMC Perle Cotton No. 12 310 Black, split back stitch and back stitch
- DMC Perle Cotton No. 8, 743 Yellow, 741 Orange, and Blanc White, satin stitch

B. Candy Buckets
- DMC Perle Cotton No. 12 310 Black, split back stitch, back stitch, and satin stitch
- Gütermann Sew-all Thread 000 Black, back stitch

C. Candy and Lollipops
- DMC Perle Cotton No. 12 310 Black, back stitch
- DMC Perle Cotton No. 8 743 Yellow, 741 Orange, and Blanc White, satin stitch, back stitch, and woven wheel stitch

D. Embellishments
- Mill Hill Petite Glass Beads 42014 Black, stitched on with Gütermann Sew-all Thread 800 White
- Mill Hill Petite Glass Beads 02034 Autumn Flame, stitched on with Gütermann Sew-all Thread 800 White and 000 Black
- Miyuki size 11 seed beads 422 Opaque Yellow Luster and 402 Opaque White, stitched on with Gütermann Sew-all Thread 800 White

Projects

Instructions

1. Prepare your embroidery hoop, and transfer the Candy Corn Bats pattern onto the fabric using your chosen transfer method.
2. Paint the jack-o'-lantern candy bucket using the Orange watercolor pencil, and paint the cat candy bucket using the Black watercolor pencil.
3. Using DMC Perle Cotton (No. 8, 743 Yellow, 741 Orange, and Blanc White), fill the bats' wing sections, bodies, and ears in with satin stitch, referencing the stitch guide image for where each thread color should go.
4. Outline the edges of the bats with split back stitch using DMC Perle Cotton (No. 12 310 Black).
5. Outline both candy buckets with split back stitch and/or back stitch using DMC Perle Cotton (No. 12 310 Black), and add the jack-o'-lantern bucket features in the same thread using satin stitch and small back stitches.
6. Stitch the cat bucket nose and mouth with some small back stitches in DMC Perle Cotton (No. 12 310 Black). Add some single, straight back stitches to make the cat bucket whiskers using Gütermann Sew-all Thread (000 Black).
7. Outline the edges of the candy and candy corn pieces with back stitch using DMC Perle Cotton (No. 12 310 Black).
8. Using DMC Perle Cotton (No. 8, 743 Yellow, 741 Orange, and Blanc White) fill in the candy and candy corn pieces with satin stitch, referencing the stitch guide image for where each thread color should go.
9. Stitch the lollipops with woven wheel stitch using DMC Perle Cotton (No. 8 743 Yellow and 741 Orange). Stitch two of the woven wheels using the Yellow thread and two using the Orange thread, then outline all four in DMC Perle Cotton (No. 12 310 Black) in back stitch, adding a single long back stitch for the lollipop sticks.

TIP: *If you don't want to stitch the lollipops using woven wheel stitch, you can use a combination of paint and stitching. At step 2, paint the lollipops with Orange and Cadmium Yellow watercolor pencils. At step 9, add some back stitch detail on top in DMC Perle Cotton (No. 8, 743 Yellow, 741 Orange, and Blanc White) and outline them in the 310 Black thread. You can see the lollipops stitched in this way in the stitch guide image.*

10. For each bat's eyes, add two Mill Hill Petite Glass Beads (42014 Black) stitched on with Gütermann Sew-all Thread (800 White).

11. Add a pair of eyes to the cat candy bucket using two Mill Hill Petite Glass Beads (02034 Autumn Flame) stitched on with Gütermann Sew-all Thread (000 Black).

12. Stitch some Mill Hill Petite Glass Beads (02034 Autumn Flame) and Miyuki size 11 seed beads (422 Opaque Yellow Luster and 402 Opaque White) in the background with Gütermann Sew-all Thread (800 White). Reference the stitch guide image and pattern template for where to place each bead.

13. Finish the back of your hoop in your chosen method, and remove any remaining visible transfer lines from the front of your work with the heat from a hair dryer.

148　　　　　　　　　　　　　　　　Projects

AUTUMNAL WITCH HAT PATTERN

When I think of Halloween, I always associate it with witches flying across a full moon on their broomsticks, accompanied by their black cat familiars. I have an early childhood memory of the witch costume my mum made me, consisting of a homemade black satin cape, a broomstick, and a paper witch hat decorated with silver stars and spiders. I—the height of trick or treating fashion. The Autumnal Witch Hat pattern combines my childhood memory with my favorite season, autumn. I love the crisp air, crunching through fallen leaves, and the anticipation that spooky season is just around the corner!

Materials List

- Cotton calico fabric (8-inch square)
- Flexi embroidery hoop (4-inch round; I used a Siesta imitation light wood grain hoop)
- Pattern transfer and transfer tools
- Watercolor painting tools
- Watercolor pencils (Orange, Deep Red, Brown, Olive Green, Terracotta, and Black)
- DMC Perle Cotton No. 12 (310 Black)
- DMC Perle Cotton No. 8 (904 Green)
- Gütermann Sew-all Thread (800 White and 000 Black)
- DMC Diamant Grandé metallic thread (G3821 Gold and G317 Grey)
- Kreinik Very Fine Braid (221 Antique Gold)
- Kreinik Blending Filament (032 Pearl)
- Mill Hill Petite Glass Beads (42033 Autumn Flame and 42014 Black)
- Mill Hill Glass Seed Beads (02011 Victorian Gold and 02054 Brilliant Shamrock)
- Miyuki size 15 seed beads (1053 Galvanized Yellow Gold)
- Miyuki size 8 seed beads (1053 Galvanized Yellow Gold and 1017 Silver Lined Emerald)
- Embroidery scissors
- Embroidery needle (size 5)
- Beading needle (size 10)
- Tapestry needle (size 24)

Stitch Guide

A. Witch Hat
- DMC Perle Cotton No. 12 310 Black, split back stitch and back stitch
- DMC Diamant Grandé metallic thread G3821 Gold, satin stitch

B. Pumpkin, Acorn, and Oak Leaf
- DMC Perle Cotton No. 12 310 Black, split back stitch and back stitch
- DMC Perle Cotton No. 8 904 Green, back stitch

C. Bat
- DMC Perle Cotton No. 12 310 Black, split back stitch, satin stitch and woven picot stitch
- DMC Diamant Grandé metallic thread G317 Grey, satin stitch

D. Ghost
   - DMC Perle Cotton No. 12 310 Black, split back stitch and satin stitch
   - Kreinik Blending Filament 032 Pearl, back stitch
E. Stars
   - Kreinik Very Fine Braid 221 Antique Gold, single stitch stars
F. Embellishments
   - Mill Hill Petite Glass Beads 42033 Autumn Flame, stitched on with Gütermann Sew-all Thread 000 Black
   - Mill Hill Petite Glass Beads 42014 Black, stitched on with Gütermann Sew-all Thread 000 Black
   - Miyuki size 15 seed beads 1053 Galvanized Yellow Gold, stitched on with Gütermann Sew-all Thread 800 White
   - Mill Hill Glass Seed Beads 02011 Victorian Gold and 02054 Brilliant Shamrock, stitched on with Gütermann Sew-all Thread 800 White
   - Miyuki size 8 seed beads 1053 Galvanized Yellow Gold and 1017 Silver Lined Emerald, stitched on with Gütermann Sew-all Thread 800 White

Instructions

1. Prepare your embroidery hoop, and transfer the Autumnal Witch Hat pattern onto the fabric using your chosen transfer method.
2. Paint the pumpkin using the Orange, Deep Red, and Brown watercolor pencils. First, fill the jack-o'-lantern with Orange, then blend in Deep Red in the shaded areas. Wait for this section to dry, then fill the stalk with the Brown watercolor pencil. Reference the pattern in the back of the book if you need help with the shading placement.
3. Paint the oak leaf using the Olive Green watercolor pencil, then paint the acorn using the Brown and Terracotta watercolor pencils. Add the Brown at the base of the acorn, and the Terracotta at the top.
4. When your paint has dried, fill in the witch hat with the Black watercolor pencil, layering extra tint in the shaded areas. Again, referencing the pattern in the back of the book will help with the shading placement.
5. Outline the pumpkin, acorn, oak leaf, and witch hat in DMC Perle Cotton (No. 12 310 Black) using split back stitch and back stitch for the straight lines on the edges of the witch hat and pumpkin. Then, stitch the vines at the top and bottom of the pumpkin in DMC Perle Cotton (No. 8 904 Green) using back stitch.

6. Using satin stitch, fill in the small areas between the acorn, oak leaf, and pumpkin with DMC Diamant Grandé metallic thread (G3821 Gold).
7. Outline the ghost in split back stitch with DMC Perle Cotton (No. 12 310 Black), and add the ghost mouth with the same thread in satin stitch.
8. Fill in the ghost with back stitch using Kreinik Blending Filament (032 Pearl).
9. Stitch the stars in the background with single straight overlapping stitches using Kreinik Very Fine Braid (221 Antique Gold).
10. Using DMC Diamant Grandé metallic thread (G317 Grey), fill the bat wing sections with satin stitch. Next, fill the bat's body with satin stitch using DMC Perle Cotton (No. 12 310 Black).
11. Outline the edges of the bat wings and body with split back stitch using DMC Perle Cotton (No. 12 310 Black).
12. Make two woven picot stitches for the bat ears using DMC Perle Cotton (No. 12 310 Black).
13. For the ghost eyes, add two Mill Hill Petite Glass Beads (42014 Black), stitching them on with Gütermann Sew-all Thread (000 Black).
14. For the bat eyes, add two Mill Hill Petite Glass Beads (42033 Autumn Flame), stitching them on with Gütermann Sew-all Thread (000 Black).
15. Stitch the Miyuki size 15 seed beads (1053 Galvanized Yellow Gold) in the background with Gütermann Sew-all Thread (800 White).
16. At the base of the pumpkin add two Mill Hill Glass Seed Beads (02011 Victorian Gold) and one each of the Mill Hill Glass Seed Beads (02054 Brilliant Shamrock) and Miyuki size 8 seed beads (1053 Galvanized Yellow Gold and 1017 Silver Lined Emerald). Reference the stitch guide image and pattern template for where to place each bead.
17. Finish the back of your hoop in your chosen method, and remove any remaining visible transfer lines from the front of your work with the heat from a hair dryer.

TIP: *I love inventing different facial expressions for my jack-o'-lanterns and pumpkins. Feel free to get creative and add different expressions to your jack-o'-lanterns too!*

152 Projects

SEASONS CREEPINGS WREATH PATTERN

Hanging a wreath is a very popular decorating tradition during the festive season. In fact, many people hang wreaths all year round decorated to match holidays and seasons. So, I thought, why not make the traditional Christmas wreath a little spooky? That's how my Seasons Creepings Wreath pattern was born. Adorned with bats and delicate bead ornaments, the design features a painted festive red bow and an appliqué skull. Hang this spooky wreath in your home to bring some frightfully festive cheer!

Materials List

- Cotton calico fabric (7-inch square)
- Flexi embroidery hoop (3.5-inch round; I used a Siesta imitation light wood grain hoop)
- Pattern transfer and transfer tools
- Watercolor painting tools
- Watercolor pencils (Deep Red and White)
- DMC Perle Cotton No. 12 (310 Black)
- DMC Perle Cotton No. 8 (319 Green)
- DMC Diamant metallic thread (D310 Black)
- DMC Diamant Grandé metallic thread (G317 Grey)
- Gütermann Sew-all Thread (800 White and 000 Black)
- White felt (small piece)
- Mill Hill Antique Glass Beads (03049 Rich Red)
- Mill Hill Glass Seed Beads (00557 Old Gold)
- Miyuki size 8 seed beads (1053 Galvanized Yellow Gold)
- Miyuki size 15 seed beads (0181 Galvanized Silver)
- Embroidery scissors
- Embroidery needle (size 5)
- Beading needle (size 10)

Stitch Guide

A. Wreath Branches
  - DMC Perle Cotton No. 12 319 Green, split back stitch
B. Appliqué Felt Skull Bow
  - Gütermann Sew-all Thread 800 White, whip stitch
  - DMC Perle Cotton No. 12 310 Black, split back stitch, back stitch, and satin stitch
  - Gütermann Sew-all Thread 000 Black, back stitch

C. Bats
- DMC Perle Cotton No. 12 310 Black, split back stitch and satin stitch
- DMC Diamant Grandé metallic thread G317 Grey, satin stitch
- DMC Diamant metallic thread D310 Black, satin stitch

D. Embellishments
- Miyuki size 15 seed beads 0181 Galvanized Silver, stitched on with Gütermann Sew-all Thread 000 Black
- Miyuki size 8 seed beads 1053 Galvanized Yellow Gold, stitched on with Gütermann Sew-all Thread 800 White
- Mill Hill Glass Seed Beads 00557 Old Gold, stitched on with Gütermann Sew-all Thread 800 White
- Mill Hill Antique Glass Beads 03049 Rich Red, stitched on with Gütermann Sew-all Thread 800 White

Projects

Instructions

1. Prepare your embroidery hoop, and transfer the Seasons Creepings Wreath pattern onto the fabric using your chosen transfer method.
2. Paint the bow using the Deep Red watercolor pencil, adding extra Deep Red in the shaded areas and White to add highlights. Reference the pattern in the back of the book if you need help with the shading placement.
3. Trace the shape of the skull onto the piece of white felt and cut it out with your embroidery scissors.
4. Attach the felt skull onto the fabric in the middle of the bow using whip stitch and a length of Gütermann Sew-all Thread (800 White).
5. Using DMC Perle Cotton (No. 12 310 Black), stitch around the edge of the skull in back stitch, then add the skull features using single back stitches and satin stitch.
6. Outline the bow in DMC Perle Cotton (No. 12 310 Black) with split back stitch, adding the fine line details in Gütermann Sew-all Thread (000 Black) with back stitch.
7. Stitch the wreath branches using DMC Perle Cotton (No. 12 319 Green) with split back stitch.
8. Using DMC Diamant Grandé metallic thread (G317 Grey), fill the bats' wing sections in with satin stitch. Then fill the bodies of the bats in with satin stitch using DMC Diamant metallic thread (D310 Black).
9. Outline the edges of the bats' wings and bodies with split back stitch using DMC Perle Cotton (No. 12 310 Black).
10. For each bat, add two Miyuki size 15 seed beads (0181 Galvanized Silver) to make their eyes, stitching them on with Gütermann Sew-all Thread (000 Black).

TIP: *If you want, experiment with different shades of green thread to stitch the wreath branches, use different colored beads, or even change the color of the bow. Experimenting is one of my favorite parts of the creative process!*

11. Around the wreath, stitch on some Miyuki size 8 seed beads (1053 Galvanized Yellow Gold), Mill Hill Glass Seed Beads (00557 Old Gold), and Mill Hill Antique Glass Beads (03049 Rich Red), attaching them with Gütermann Sew-all Thread 800 White. Reference the stitch guide image and pattern template for where to place each bead.
12. Finish the back of your hoop in your chosen method, and remove any remaining visible transfer lines from the front of your work with the heat from a hair dryer.

Projects

158 Projects

CODE ORANGE HAUNTED HOUSE PATTERN

Haunted houses were some of the first designs I made when I launched my embroidery business. I've probably stitched a haunted house in every color of the rainbow, but my favorite ones are always the perfect shade of Halloween orange! Why is this pattern called the Code Orange Haunted House? Amongst the Halloween community, the term *Code Orange* is used as an alert for when Halloween starts appearing in shops or homes. You wouldn't want to miss out on any of the Halloween fun, so stitch this pattern up quick!

Materials List

- Cotton calico fabric (7 x 9 inches)
- Flexi embroidery hoop (4-x-5.5-inch oval; I used a Siesta imitation light wood grain hoop)
- Pattern transfer and transfer tools
- Watercolor painting tools
- Watercolor pencils (Orange, Deep Red, and Black)
- DMC Perle Cotton No. 12 (310 Black)
- DMC Diamant metallic thread (D310 Black)
- DMC Diamant Grandé metallic thread (G317 Grey and G3821 Gold)
- Gütermann Sew-all Thread (800 White and 000 Black)
- Gütermann Sulky Metallic Thread (7023 Silver)
- Kreinik Blending Filament (032 Pearl)
- White felt (small piece)
- Mill Hill Glass Seed Beads (00557 Old Gold)
- Mill Hill Petite Glass Beads (42014 Black)
- Embroidery scissors
- Embroidery needle (size 5)
- Beading needle (size 10)

Stitch Guide

A. Haunted House and Jack-o'-lantern
   - DMC Perle Cotton No. 12 310 Black, split back stitch and back stitch
   - DMC Diamant metallic thread D310 Black, split back stitch
   - DMC Diamant Grandé metallic thread G3821 Gold, satin stitch and back stitch
   - Gütermann Sulky Metallic Thread 7023 Silver, back stitch

B. Appliqué Felt Skull
- DMC Perle Cotton No. 12 310 Black, back stitch and satin stitch
- Gütermann Sew-all Thread 800 White, whip stitch

C. Bats
- DMC Perle Cotton No. 12 310 Black, back stitch
- DMC Diamant Grandé metallic thread G317 Grey, satin stitch and back stitch

D. Ghost
- DMC Perle Cotton No. 12 310 Black, split back stitch and satin stitch
- Kreinik Blending Filament 032 Pearl, back stitch

E. Crescent Moon and Stars
- DMC Diamant Grandé metallic thread G3821 Gold, satin stitch and back stitch
- DMC Perle Cotton No. 12 310 Black, split back stitch

F. Embellishments
- Mill Hill Petite Glass Beads 42014 Black, stitched on with Gütermann Sew-all Thread 000 Black
- Mill Hill Glass Seed Beads 00557 Old Gold, stitched on with Gütermann Sew-all Thread 800 White

Instructions

1. Prepare your embroidery hoop, and transfer the Code Orange Haunted House pattern onto the fabric using your chosen transfer method.
2. Start by painting the main section of the haunted house using the Orange watercolor pencil, blending Deep Red into the shaded areas. Next, paint the little jack-o'-lantern in the window, also in Orange, adding the Brown watercolor pencil to the jack-o'-lantern stalk
3. When the Orange sections are dry, use the Black watercolor pencil to fill in the haunted house roof, door, and bay window, referencing the pattern in the back of the book to see where to add the shading.
4. Trace the shape of the skull onto the piece of white felt and cut it out with your embroidery scissors.
5. Attach the felt skull at the top of the door using whip stitch with a length of Gütermann Sew-all Thread (800 White).
6. Using DMC Perle Cotton (No. 12 310 Black), stitch around the edge of the skull in back stitch, then add the skull features using single back stitches and satin stitch.
7. Outline the little jack-o'-lantern in the window in DMC Perle Cotton (No. 12 310 Black) using split back stitch. Add in the features with some tiny back stitches.
8. Using DMC Diamant Grandé metallic thread (G3821 Gold) fill in all the windows using satin stitch, then outline them in DMC Perle Cotton (No. 12 310 Black) using split back stitch.
9. Fill the long section at the base of the roof and the sections at the tops of the rooftop windows with DMC Diamant metallic thread (D310 Black), stitching in lines of split back stitch. Reference the pattern template for the directional stitch lines. After you fill in these sections, outline them in DMC Perle Cotton (No. 12 310 Black) using split back stitch.
10. Add the gold detail on the haunted house door and along the top of the bay window in DMC Diamant Grandé metallic thread (G3821 Gold) with single back stitches.

11. Outline the rest of the haunted house in DMC Perle Cotton (No. 12 310 Black) using split back stitch, adding the lines at the base of the roof in single back stitches.
12. Stitch the line detail on the haunted house roof with Gütermann Sulky Metallic Thread (7023 Silver) in back stitch.'
13. Using DMC Diamant Grandé metallic thread (G317 Grey), fill the bats' wing sections in with satin stitch. Then stitch the bodies of the bats with some small single back stitches using DMC Perle Cotton (No. 12 310 Black).
14. Outline the edges of the bat wings with single back stitches using DMC Perle Cotton (No. 12 310 Black), then stitch two small back stitches to make the bat eyes with DMC Diamant Grandé metallic thread (G317 Grey). As these bats are very small, you don't need to outline the bottom of the wings.
15. Outline the ghost in split back stitch with DMC Perle Cotton (No. 12 310 Black) and add the ghost mouth with the same thread in satin stitch.
16. Fill in the ghost with back stitch using Kreinik Blending Filament (032 Pearl).
17. Fill the crescent moon using satin stitch method two with DMC Diamant Grandé metallic thread (G3821 Gold), then outline in DMC Perle Cotton (No. 12 310 Black) with split back stitch.
18. Stitch the stars in the background with single straight overlapping stitches using DMC Diamant Grandé metallic thread (G3821 Gold).
19. For the ghost eyes, add two Mill Hill Petite Glass Beads (42014 Black); stitch them on with Gütermann Sew-all Thread (000 Black).
20. Stitch the Mill Hill Glass Seed Beads (00557 Old Gold) in the background with Gütermann Sew-all Thread (800 White).
21. Finish the back of your hoop in your chosen method, and remove any remaining visible transfer lines from the front of your work with the heat from a hair dryer.

TIPS

- *I satin stitch the tops and bottoms of the haunted house windows as separate sections to keep my stitches short and neat.*
- *After you outline your areas of satin stitch, you may be left with some small gaps between the outline stitching and the edges of the satin stitch. Just fill any gaps with your satin stitch thread.*

Projects

CRYSTAL GAZING GHOST PATTERN

I've always been intrigued by fortune telling and divination, practices that seek to uncover the secrets of the unknown. A lot of my university projects were inspired by these topics, and my work continues to be inspired by all things mysterious and witchy to this day. The Crystal Gazing Ghost pattern pays homage to the mystical realms between the veil and features a little ghost and bat with a fortune teller's crystal ball, as well as a delicate red rose to represent my passion for this topic. Sequins fill the crystal ball to give it a shimmering ethereal quality.

Materials List

- Cotton calico fabric (7-inch square)
- Flexi embroidery hoop (3.5-inch round; I used a Siesta imitation light wood grain hoop)
- Pattern transfer and transfer tools
- Watercolor painting tools
- Watercolor pencils (Deep Red, White, and Purple)
- DMC Perle Cotton No. 12 (310 Black)
- DMC Perle Cotton No. 8 (319 Green and 310 Black)
- DMC Diamant Grandé metallic thread (G3821 Gold and G317 Grey)
- Gütermann Sew-all Thread (800 White and 000 Black)
- White felt (small piece; I used white felt with a glitter finish)
- Mill Hill Glass Seed Beads (00557 Old Gold)
- Mill Hill Petite Glass Beads (42014 Black)
- Trimits 5mm transparent cup sequins
- Embroidery scissors
- Embroidery needle (size 5)
- Beading needle (size 10)

Stitch Guide

A. Crystal Ball
- DMC Perle Cotton No. 12 310 Black, split back stitch and back stitch
- DMC Diamant Grandé metallic thread G3821 Gold, split back stitch

B. Appliqué Felt Skull
- Gütermann Sew-all Thread 800 White, whip stitch
- DMC Perle Cotton No. 12 310 Black, back stitch and satin stitch

C. Rose
- DMC Perle Cotton No. 12 310 Black, split back stitch
- DMC Perle Cotton No. 8 319 green, split back stitch, back stitch, and leaf stitch
- Gütermann Sew-all Thread 000 Black, back stitch

D. Bat
- DMC Perle Cotton No. 12 310 Black, back stitch
- DMC Perle Cotton No. 8 310 Black, satin stitch
- DMC Diamant Grandé metallic thread G317 Grey, satin stitch and back stitch

E. Ghost
- DMC Perle Cotton No. 12 310 Black, split back stitch and satin stitch
- Kreinik Blending Filament 032 Pearl, back stitch

F. Stars
- DMC Diamant Grandé metallic thread G3821 Gold, back stitch

Projects

6. Embellishments
   - Trimits 5mm transparent cup sequins, stitched on with Gütermann Sew-all Thread 800 White
   - Mill Hill Glass Seed Beads 00557 Old Gold, stitched on with Gütermann Sew-all Thread 800 White
   - Mill Hill Petite Glass Beads 42014 Black, stitched on with Gütermann Sew-all Thread 000 Black

Instructions

1. Prepare your embroidery hoop, and transfer the Crystal Gazing Ghost pattern onto the fabric using your chosen transfer method.
2. Start by painting the rose using the Deep Red watercolor pencil, adding a touch of White to highlight the edges of the petals.
3. Use the Purple watercolor pencil to add the detail on the crystal ball, referencing the pattern in the back of the book on where to place this detail.
4. Trace the shape of the skull onto the piece of white felt, and cut it out with your embroidery scissors.
5. Attach the felt skull onto the fabric inside the crystal ball using whip stitch with a length of Gütermann Sew-all Thread (800 White).
6. Using DMC Perle Cotton (No. 12 310 Black), stitch around the edge of the skull in back stitch, then add the skull features using single back stitches and satin stitch.
7. Using DMC Diamant Grandé metallic thread (G3821 Gold) fill in the base of the crystal ball with lines of split back stitch, referencing the pattern template for the directional stitch lines. Don't worry about leaving a gap for the rose stem or leaves, as you'll be stitching this on top later.
8. Outline the crystal ball in split back stitch with DMC Perle Cotton (No. 12 310 Black), adding the lines at the base of the crystal ball with single back stitches.
9. Outline the rose petals in split back stitch with DMC Perle Cotton (No. 12 310 Black), then add the fine detail lines on the petals with single back stitches in Gütermann Sew-all Thread (000 Black).
10. Stitch the rose stem in split back stitch with DMC Perle Cotton (No. 8 319 Green), adding some small single back stitches to create the thorns along the stem. Using the same thread, stitch the leaves using leaf stitch, referencing the pattern template for the directional stitch lines if you need to.

11. Using DMC Diamant Grandé metallic thread (G317 Grey), fill in the bat wing sections with satin stitch. Next, stitch the body of the bat with satin stitch using DMC Perle Cotton (No. 8 310 Black).
12. Outline the edges of the bat wings with single back stitches using DMC Perle Cotton (No. 12 310 Black), then stitch two small back stitches to make the bat eyes with DMC Diamant Grandé metallic thread (G317 Grey).
13. Outline the ghost in split back stitch with DMC Perle Cotton (No. 12 310 Black), and add the ghost mouth with the same thread in satin stitch.
14. Fill the ghost with back stitch using Kreinik Blending Filament (032 Pearl).
15. Stitch the stars in the background with back stitch using DMC Diamant Grandé metallic thread (G3821 Gold).
16. For the ghost eyes, add two Mill Hill Petite Glass Beads (42014 Black), stitching them on with Gütermann Sew-all Thread (000 Black).
17. Stitch the Mill Hill Glass Seed Beads (00557 Old Gold) in the background with Gütermann Sew-all Thread (800 White).
18. Fill the crystal ball in with the Trimits 5mm transparent cup sequins, stitching them on with Gütermann Sew-all Thread (800 White) following the method for stitching a group of sequins.
19. Finish the back of your hoop in your chosen method, and remove any remaining visible transfer lines from the front of your work with the heat from a hair dryer.

TIP: *When you're stitching on your sequins, don't worry if they slightly cover your outline stitching. You can trim the sequin edges down if you like using your embroidery scissors, just be careful not to cut any of the stitching you've already done and keep the center of your sequin intact so it stays secure on the fabric.*

Acknowledgements

I've had so much fun writing this book of spooky embroidery patterns for you all, and I want to take a moment now to thank all the lovely people who have not just been a part of this venture but have been there with me from the start.

Firstly, I want to thank my wonderful editor Kelly, who reached out to me with this amazing opportunity of working on a book of spooky Halloween embroidery patterns with her and the Rocky Nook team. I am so grateful that you believed in me and my work and that I could undertake this new journey of authoring a book. Your help and support along the way have been invaluable, and it's been an absolute pleasure to work with you. I can't thank you and the amazing team at Rocky Nook enough.

To Jake, my beloved husband, thank you for your never-ending love and support. You are my rock and inspire me to keep reaching for my dreams every single day. You have been quite literally by my side for every single art market, exhibition, and artistic venture since the day we met. I am so grateful to have shared all this with you so far and know you'll continue to be by my side for all the adventures to come.

To my wonderful parents, thank you for your endless love and support and for always encouraging me to follow a creative path. You have always inspired and nurtured my creativity, encouraging me to draw, make, and explore, and I will be forever grateful for this.

To my sisters Rachel and Rowena, thank you for always being as strange as I am and for all the happy and hilarious memories we've shared together.

To Kat and Fi, my best friends for life, I am so lucky to have met you both at university, and to have shared all the ups and downs life has thrown at us. Thank you for always being there for me. It's an absolute joy to have two like-minded, artistic, and weird souls in my life, and I love you both dearly.

To my grandparents, thank you for all the wonderful and happy memories I have growing up with you and for shaping me into the person I am today.

And finally, thank you to each and every one of you who supports me and my spooky work in any way, shape, or form. I wouldn't be where I am today without your support, and I'm so grateful that I get to make and share my spooky art with you.

About the Author

Laura is an artist/maker with a love for cats, spooky films, heavy metal music, and sewing. She lives in Wales with her husband, son, and two mischievous cats, Salem and Loki. A huge lover of Halloween and everything spooky (all year round!), Laura runs her embroidery business, Cat & Magpie, from her home.

Laura has loved to draw and paint from a young age, and she quickly found a passion for textiles and fiber arts. In her teenage years, she began to make fairy dolls using her mum's stash of threads, yarn, and fabric, incorporating tiny trinkets and bits of broken jewelry to give each fairy a unique personality. She even went on to sell some of her fairy dolls in a local gift shop and partake in local craft markets.

Laura continued to pursue her love for all things creative during her time at college, studying photography, art, and fashion textiles. She then went on to university to study art and textiles, where she achieved a first-class honors degree in contemporary textile practice followed by a distinction in her master's degree of fine art. During her time at university, she worked alongside other creatives and learned from some of the best and most inspiring tutors and artists she could ask for, pushing the boundaries of her artistic practice and truly shaping how she works as an artist today. Laura was able to explore many creative avenues during her studies, including bronze and resin casting, ceramics, woodwork, printing, and more, but her main passion always came back to embroidery.

After finishing her university studies in 2014, Laura continued to create in her spare time, opening an Etsy shop to sell her embroidery work, as well as handmade jewelry. She also took part in various art exhibitions and craft shows. In summer 2013, her first solo exhibition, *Occulta Scientia*, showcased her collection of embroideries and stitched artworks inspired by *Knowledge of the Hidden*. In 2014, she then collaborated with two of her fellow artists on a group art exhibition called *Intertwined Narratives* at the newly refurbished Penarth Pier in Wales. Two years later, she collaborated with her fellow artist and best friend on *ConcealedRevealed*, an art installation of stitched and gilded vintage postcards displayed in a listed Edwardian cloakroom in Bristol.

At the end of 2019, Laura took the leap to focus on Cat & Magpie full time, and on Instagram, she discovered a wonderful community of fellow Halloween lovers that shared her passion of keeping things a little spooky all year round! Laura now regularly releases spooky embroidery collections throughout the year and takes part in the online Darksome Art and Craft Market, which showcases an array of spooky art and craft.

In August 2023, Laura and her husband Jake welcomed their son Finn to the family. Although this meant having a little less time to quietly stitch away, Laura still created small collections of spooky embroideries, as well as custom embroidery projects. While thinking about where to take her business next, Laura was surprised and excited by the opportunity to collaborate with the wonderful Rocky Nook team on a book of spooky Halloween embroidery patterns. Laura had been thinking about making her embroidery designs into patterns for a while, and she was (and is) thrilled to be able to share her work and knowledge with you in this new chapter of her artistic career.

PATTERN TEMPLATES

SPOOKY STITCH SAMPLER

TRACEABLE PATTERN TEMPLATE

This pattern is to scale. Trace this image, and position it in the center of your embroidery hoop to transfer it to your fabric. This pattern template also includes paint shading guides in gray, embellishment placement in orange, and directional stitch lines in lilac.

VALLOWEEN TEACUP BAT

TRACEABLE PATTERN TEMPLATE

This pattern is to scale. Trace this image, and position it in the center of your embroidery hoop to transfer it to your fabric. This pattern template also includes paint shading guides in gray, embellishment placement in orange, and directional stitch lines in lilac.

HAUNTED HOLLY

TRACEABLE PATTERN TEMPLATE

This pattern is to scale. Trace this image, and position it in the center of your embroidery hoop to transfer it to your fabric. This pattern template also includes paint shading guides in gray and embellishment placement in orange.

TRICK OR TREAT CUPCAKE

TRACEABLE PATTERN TEMPLATE

This pattern is to scale. Trace this image, and position it in the center of your embroidery hoop to transfer it to your fabric. This pattern template also includes paint shading guides in gray, embellishment placement in orange, and directional stitch lines in lilac.

SPOOKY BLUE BOO-QUET

TRACEABLE PATTERN TEMPLATE

This pattern is to scale. Trace this image, and position it in the center of your embroidery hoop to transfer it to your fabric. This pattern template also includes paint shading guides in gray, embellishment placement in orange, and directional stitch lines in lilac.

SUMMER GOTH ICE CREAM

TRACEABLE PATTERN TEMPLATE

This pattern is to scale. Trace this image, and position it in the center of your embroidery hoop to transfer it to your fabric. This pattern template also includes paint shading guides in gray, embellishment placement in orange, and directional stitch lines in lilac.

HALLOWEEN PUMPKIN CAT

TRACEABLE PATTERN TEMPLATE

This pattern is to scale. Trace this image, and position it in the center of your embroidery hoop to transfer it to your fabric. This pattern template also includes paint shading guides in gray, embellishment placement in orange, and directional stitch lines in lilac.

KRAMPUS KITTY

TRACEABLE PATTERN TEMPLATE

This pattern is to scale. Trace this image, and position it in the center of your embroidery hoop to transfer it to your fabric. This pattern template also includes paint shading guides in gray and embellishment placement in orange.

HAUNTED GARDEN GHOST

TRACEABLE PATTERN TEMPLATE

This pattern is to scale. Trace this image, and position it in the center of your embroidery hoop to transfer it to your fabric. This pattern template also includes paint shading guides in gray, embellishment placement in orange, and directional stitch lines in lilac.

CANDY CORN BATS

TRACEABLE PATTERN TEMPLATE

This pattern is to scale. Trace this image, and position it in the center of your embroidery hoop to transfer it to your fabric. This pattern template also includes paint shading guides in gray, embellishment placement in orange, and directional stitch lines in lilac.

AUTUMNAL WITCH HAT

TRACEABLE PATTERN TEMPLATE

This pattern is to scale. Trace this image, and position it in the center of your embroidery hoop to transfer it to your fabric. This pattern template also includes paint shading guides in gray, embellishment placement in orange, and directional stitch lines in lilac.

SEASONS CREEPINGS WREATH

TRACEABLE PATTERN TEMPLATE

This pattern is to scale. Trace this image, and position it in the center of your embroidery hoop to transfer it to your fabric. This pattern template also includes paint shading guides in gray, embellishment placement in orange, and directional stitch lines in lilac.